THE LANGUAGE OF MONEY

Also by William Davis

Three Years Hard Labour
Merger Mania

THE LANGUAGE OF MONEY

An Irreverent Dictionary of Business & Finance

WILLIAM DAVIS

1973

Houghton Mifflin Company Boston

First Printing c

First American Edition

Copyright © 1972, 1973 by William Davis
All rights reserved. No part of this work may be
reproduced or transmitted in any form by any means,
electronic or mechanical, including photocopying
and recording, or by any information storage or retrieval
system, without permission in writing from the publisher.
ISBN: 0-395-13999-6
Library of Congress Catalog Card Number: 72-2281
Printed in the United States of America

A selection from this book has appeared in *Money*.

Preambulatory Inception Brief

The point is that the thing for Mr. Jenkins to think of, *inter alia*, in making his judgment, and for observers to have in mind in judging it, is the whole of the V-shape above the probable range of payments outcomes, not just its base or the intersection with the point of greatest probability.

Peter Jay,
Economics Editor of *The London Times*

The wider band system therefore risks being either too rigid or too volatile. It may have a double disadvantage. It gives perhaps excessive immediate flexibility, with scope for "normal" variations in exchange rates that if left to themselves may be inappropriate for the desired correction of the payments balance, and yet involve significant uncertainty to traders and investors. At the same time, unless it leans significantly on parity changes which will introduce their own disturbances, it has inadequate continuing flexibility.

Fred Hirsch, author of
Money International

Do they *have* to talk like that? Is it impossible to discuss money in simple language? There are people who have made a million — and more — without ever finding out what wider band system, business cycle, parity, floating, or crawling peg means. So, I suppose, the short answer is "No."

Every trade, or profession, has its jargon. Even the man whose life is devoted to selling baked beans will, on occasion, use words and phrases which outsiders do not understand. Scientists, including economists, have a particularly strong case for using their own special language, their own precise modes of calculation and communication. Some things sound complex because they *are* complex. Jargon, moreover, offers comfort and security. It's safer to use terms accepted by fellow experts than to lay oneself open to a charge of oversimplification. If outsiders want to enter one's world — well, let them learn the language.

There is also the argument, of course, that you have to sound complex to impress. Economics is a comparatively young science, and economists have never been quite sure of their place in the academic and business worlds. Theirs is an inexact science, and there is a natural temptation to look down on it. At the universities, economists are often held in low regard. In business, they are frequently dismissed as daydreamers who couldn't sell a pair of shoes, or run a company, in a month of Sundays. This is one reason why the jargon of economics is worse than most. It takes considerable skill, moreover, to keep up with it. There's an old joke, well known among economists, about the student who went back to his university, after twenty years, and found that the examination papers still asked exactly the same questions. "Ah, but you see," his old professor explained, "in economics the questions stay the same, but we change the answers."

Economists themselves often make fun of their profession's lack of contact with reality. Milton Friedman, the Chicago economist, once told an appreciative audience of fellow experts the following story: "A chemist, physicist, and

PREAMBULATORY INCEPTION BRIEF

an economist were stranded on a desert island. They had nothing but canned food, and no can opener. The chemist said that if they lit a fire, he could calculate the degree of heat needed for the cans to burst open. The physicist said that, if the chemist did that, he could calculate the trajectory of the food as it shot out of the can, so that they would be able to stand in the right place to catch it. The economist said he couldn't understand all the fuss. The answer was perfectly simple. 'Let us *assume* we have a can-opener.' "

Economists, of course, are by no means the only people who come in for this kind of mockery. Technocrats are every bit as good a target. Not long ago, a British college of technology circulated a tactical manual for use "in the battles with technological and management whizzkids" among its 330 apparently hard-pressed staff. Describing itself as a guide in "verbal one-upmanship" it consisted of thirty key nouns and adjectives deployable in conversation with technocrats. "Take any word from the first column," the authors advised, "combine it with any word in the second column — then add any word in the third column." Here is the guide:

Integrated	Management	Options
Total	Organization	Flexibility
Systemized	Monitored	Capability
Parallel	Reciprocal	Mobility
Functional	Digital	Programming
Responsive	Logic	Concept
Optical	Transitional	Time phrases
Synchronized	Incremental	Projection hardware
Compatible	Third generation	Contingency
Balanced	Policy	

If the instructions are followed, the manual claimed, "few

listeners will admit ignorance of the impressive-sounding result."

John Kenneth Galbraith, who has occasionally been attacked by his academic colleagues for writing too well, says in his book *Economics, Peace and Laughter* that clear and unambiguous statement may not be the best medium for persuasion. Had the Bible been in clear, straightforward language, he maintains, it would almost certainly have been a work of lesser influence. The archaic constructions and terminology put some special strain on the reader, so by the time he has worked his way through it all he has a vested interest in what he has read. A newspaper column is more easily dismissed. The ambiguities of the Scriptures, moreover, allow infinite debate over what is meant. I have great admiration for Professor Galbraith and I like to think he was joking, but I am sure that a lot of economists would go along with his argument. To me, though, this kind of reasoning is anathema. To defend economic jargon and ambiguity on the grounds that in order to appreciate and accept another man's case you must find it hard to understand seems to me pretentious nonsense.

Not only pretentious but, all too often, dangerous. Finance and economics are not just academic subjects, reserved for the cosy study or classroom. They do not exist to prove the validity of pet theories, but to serve the individual. Nor, for that matter, are they the exclusive preserve of an administrative elite. The days when people did as they were told have gone. A politician has to sell himself, and the theories of economists, to those whose cooperation is needed to make the theories work. You don't sell an incomes policy to the workers on the factory floor by publishing incomprehensible government papers, and lecturing them on wider band systems. The labor unions, particularly, tend to be in no mood to listen to jargon, however elegant. Governments rightly regard "wage explosions" as a menace. To the worker, though, it's simply a matter of looking after your own interests. The "corporate philosophy" is to maximize profits. Why shouldn't workers join managements in the race for bigger gains? You won't get them to change their minds unless you can convince them, in plain English, that the whole thing is certain to backfire. Bloodymindedness, fear, panic — these things cannot be measured by building economic models, yet they clearly have a major bearing in modern economic and business management.

There are, in addition, a great many people who are interested in economics by the fact that this vast area so obviously affects the fate of governments, and the future of their own jobs and business ventures. There is no reason why they should be fluent in the language of the specialist.

Many thoughtful economists accept that, in today's changed conditions, it's not enough to produce learned papers. They recognize that the very quality of postwar economics, the greater sophistication of its theoretical constructions, its much refined statistical methods, may have made economics more respected in the universities, but has tended at the same time to put it out of touch with real economic situations. Sir Alec Cairncross, a former head of the British Government's economic service, says that "economists have been insulated from industrial and commercial problems, and encouraged to apply themselves to those fascinating conundrums in which pure theory is so rich." And he has this warning for nonexperts: "Beware of being marched in bold logic by the priestly up the garden path."

His views are not, of course, shared by all of his colleagues. Some have shown increasing disgust with the whole democratic process: the mechanics of electioneering,

PREAMBULATORY INCEPTION BRIEF

the apparent stupidity of labor unions, and the reluctance of individuals to go along with schemes which, on paper, have obvious merits. These men have sought refuge in the sheltered, comforting surroundings provided by their universities. They argue that, if their schemes have not worked out as intended, it's all the fault of stupid politicians and an equally stupid electorate. Their advice to fellow experts is to concentrate on refining economic theories, and to maintain a dignified silence.

This, of course, is much the safest approach. Pretend that economics has nothing to do with real life, and no one will ever give you trouble. There are, nevertheless, people who think economics has a little more to offer. "It is not enough," says Cambridge's Graham Hallett, "to have a good idea; the practical problems of implementing it must be carefully thought out if it is in practice to do more good than harm." Any businessman could have told him that years ago, but it is nice to have it acknowledged.

The ideal solution, clearly, is for economists to acknowledge that their ideas must not only be practical but, as far as possible, comprehensible to the intelligent layman — and for the rest of us to make some effort to discover what it's all about. If this book helps, I shall be delighted. Its origins go back to my publisher's suggestion that I should write a guide to money which my Aunt Bertha could understand. Aunt Bertha is a fictional character I created for my column in the *Manchester Guardian* some years ago, as a way of making jargon understood by ordinary people. As it turned out, she quickly acquired a personality of her own, and started to express unorthodox, highly critical views on economics and finance. Today she is a very real person to many *Guardian* readers — and, I confess, to me.

I have put together a dictionary of terms used regularly by economists, specialists in international finance, accountants, financial editors, stock market dealers — and millionaires.

Some of the terms in this book will be understood only by the American reader, and this is how it should be. But finance has become more international, and I make no apology for including some terms which will be unfamiliar to Americans. Inevitably, too, some of my comments are written from a British point of view — which I hope you will find refreshing. The overall aim has been not only to translate, but to get as close as possible to what I believe to be the practical meaning of a word or phrase.

It means, very often, that my interpretation differs from the one generally accepted in the academic world. No matter; in economics, and in business, there is room for more than one version. If you are completely at home in the world of fixed parities, floating currencies, conglomerates, multinationals, invisibles, and fundamentalists you may enjoy quarreling with my interpretations. For those who want to delve more deeply, I have added a list of books which I personally have found not only useful, but enjoyable.

Inevitably, there will be terms which I have missed. No glossary can ever be complete, if only because the volume of jargon is still growing at an alarming rate. Wage-price controls and the dollar's problems in world money markets have both widened the scope. Embarrassingly high unemployment has lead to the creation of euphemisms like "disemployed" and "involuntarily leisured." People are no longer out of work—they are "resting." And, as Churchill noted many years ago, the poor are no longer the poor but "lower-income groups." Governments don't freeze a workman's wages, they "arrest increases in personal income." And they don't cut expenditure on education, they "ease the financial burden of know-how acquisition." Churchill

PREAMBULATORY INCEPTION BRIEF

once had a good deal of fun with his socialist opponents, who kept talking about "accommodation units." He said he understood they meant homes, and asked how we were in future to sing the old song "Home, Sweet Home." He then sang: "Accommodation Unit, Sweet Accommodation Unit, there's no place like our Accommodation Unit." The House of Commons cheered as he added: "I hope to live to see the British democracy spit all this rubbish from their lips."

Churchill would have been appalled, but not surprised, by the way jargon is spreading, not only in politics and economic management, but in normal business fields.

Take "management by objectives," which is being offered on a consultative basis as though it were a new discovery or some modern technology. You've read the interviews: "Since we turned over to management by objectives we have . . ." All it means is that "Since we sat down and decided to find out what we had to do to make profits . . ." Targets of achievement are as old as man, yet one has seen consultatory recommendations which advise "management by objectives" as a revolutionary policy that allows the consultant to extract high fees. There are others: cost effectiveness, cost benefit, discounted cash flow, management by committee. Shops have become "retail outlets," even when they are shops — which I accept they are not all the time. Workers' overalls are "career apparel" or "corporate clothing." One gets a completely foreign language in the product-development business and even more so in the advertising game. Many of us have sat through those overlong presentations of new products where someone starts with sententious pronouncements accompanied by slides projected on a large screen. It takes him half an hour to wade through a barrel of phrases like motivational research, consumer orientation, and aspirational undercurrents to say that his company thought they ought to bring out a new chocolate bar because they expect it to make money.

While writing this book, I was invited to attend a conference of market researchers in Amsterdam. The papers prepared for the occasion were classic exercises in mumbo jumbo. I won't weary you with samples, but it might interest you to know that, at the end of three days' talking, the conference concluded that there was "a lack of understanding of the communications process and the consequent development of irrelevant research measures." It also conceded that market researchers had been "relying on the wrong model of how advertising works" and had therefore "adopted a wrong model of the campaign planning process."

Baron Rothschild, the famous French financier, was once heard to say that he knew of only two men who really understood money — an obscure clerk in the Bank of France and one of the directors of the Bank of England. "Unfortunately," he added, "they disagree." The number of genuine experts has increased somewhat since then, but there is still an awful lot of pretense, designed chiefly to provide a veneer of professionalism. It's impossible to stop it, but next time someone tries to dazzle you with science ask him to explain, in plain English, what he's talking about. The chances are that he doesn't know either.

THE LANGUAGE OF MONEY

AD VALOREM

In business, as in law and sex, Latin words and phrases are sometimes used instead of English. This is to make the subject look more dignified and authoritative. (In sex, of course, it is a way of discussing the subject without actually mentioning the unspeakable: even Indian terms like *lingam* and *yoni* are acceptable.) *Ad valorem* means "according to value"; an *ad valorem* tax (such as stamp duty) is one levied on a percentage of value. As far as I'm concerned, the English translation would do just as well — but that would, of course, mean breaking with tradition.

Other Latin phrases you may come across include *ex gratia* ("as a matter of favor"), *a fortiori* ("with all the more force"), and *ad referendum*, a term sometimes used in connection with a contract, meaning that, although it has been signed, certain matters have been left over for consideration. There are other terms — indeed, one could go on *ad infinitum* — but they are not really vital to an understanding of your first million — unless, perhaps, you happen to be in the hands of a crooked lawyer.

AMEX
See BIG BOARD.

ANNUAL GENERAL MEETING
A yearly ritual imposed on public companies by law. The AGM is open to all stockholders, but the majority of meetings are sparsely attended and dreadfully dull. The British, on the whole, don't like complaining. It embarrasses them. So the chairman races through the agenda, accepts a vote of thanks, and rushes off to the nearest bar, relieved that the democratic process is over for another year. I have seen meetings disposed of before we've all had time to take our coats off: the legal formalities can be got through in a few minutes.

Once in a while, though, someone does make a bold attempt to hold up the proceedings. He may be a professional trying to exploit the occasion. Or a genuine, sensible chap representing a group of like-minded people. Or a crank. Cranks and eccentrics provide the most fun, though they often go too far. Midland Bank meetings used to be enlivened by a farmer in dirty gum boots, who harangued the board nonstop and, when the directors tried to terminate the meeting, leaped on the polished boardroom table and walked up and down hurling abuse at the directors. At their best eccentrics manage to puncture inflated boardroom egos. At their worst, they allow directors to uphold the British reputation for tolerance. Mostly they brighten up routine occasions.

One performer I remember with particular affection was an Irish spinster who wore the most outlandish clothes and turned up at meetings on a bicycle. At one meeting she propped up her cycle outside the door of the Dorchester and was haughtily refused admission. She eventually got in, asked many pertinent questions, and was treated with great respect by the rather terrified board. Her counterpart in America, cigar-smoking Mrs. Stross, once arrived at a United Steel meeting in a Gay Nineties costume — "dressed to match management thinking."

And an American called Lewis Dusenbery Gilbert was greeted once at an AGM by the chairman with "I wish you were dead." Gilbert applied his wealth and time entirely to championing the rights of minority stockholders, and made a national reputation as the terror of the boardrooms. The directors of Columbia Broadcasting spoke for many fellow executives when they complained: "We used to look forward to the AGMs. Now we anticipate them with dread." When Gilbert made his first appearance at the annual meeting of Ford, Henry Ford II — recognizing him sitting quietly among the other stockholders — pointed him out and said: "We missed you the last six years, Mr. Gilbert. We have been expecting you every year. We did not know what was wrong with us."

In Britain, financial journalists have fond memories of the "Gordon riots" — a succession of stormy gatherings at which stockholders and directors of Gordon Hotels hurled invectives at each other with a fervor and skill that makes today's House of Commons clashes look like mealtimes in a kindergarten. At an annual meeting of Sidney Flavel, in the late fifties, a stockholder threw something more solid — three eggs and one tomato. He later explained that this is "the only way I can show my disapproval." It wasn't the first time someone has reinforced his arguments in this way. There was, for example, a tough Yorkshire character who traveled to London for annual meetings. He always wore a cloth cap, and never took it off. On one occasion, after asking the chairman a number of questions and getting unsatisfactory answers, he stood on his chair, took off his cap, and hurled it at the unfortunate company chief. Seasoned reporters also treasure the moment when a chairman, furious at persistent interruptions from a stockbroker, picked up a stockholders' register and threw it at his tormentor.

This sort of violence is comparatively rare nowadays, but students and others with a grievance have discovered that, with reporters present, annual meetings are a good way of drawing attention to a protest. Firms with interests in South Africa, for example, now tend to find themselves harassed by antiapartheid demonstrators. Another group well placed to score are labor unionists; a single share will usually buy admission and, as long as they don't lose their tempers, they can often squeeze concessions out of an embarrassed board.

There are times, of course, when stockholders are their own worst enemy. They shout down a man when they should be backing him. Companies naturally encourage this by packing their meetings with senior employees who act as boo-leaders. Some also announce, at the earliest possible opportunity, that there is free sherry or (if the year's results look particularly bad) champagne waiting for them in an adjoining room. It seems churlish to criticize such a generous board, and anyone who tries to keep people from free booze is regarded as a cad. (Another favorite trick is to hold your annual meeting in a tiny place, far away from the big cities, which no one has ever heard of and which stockholders and financial journalists have not the slightest desire to visit.)

But perhaps the biggest problem is that professional critics — stockbrokers, accountants, bankers, and the like — frequently go over to the other side. Stockbrokers are sometimes silenced by a discreet offer of business. And it is not unusual for accountants and bankers who make a nuisance of themselves to be invited to join the board. In many cases, of course, this is the chief motive for making a fuss in the first place: it's a quick way to the top.

ANNUITY
A means of insuring that you have a regular income for the rest of your life. There are several different types of annuities, but the most common involves the payment of a lump sum in return for a fixed income each year for the rest of your life. Its appeal, obviously, is chiefly to people who have retired or are about to retire and the cost of the annuity depends on age, state of health, and other factors. The main advantage is that you know exactly where you stand. The main disadvantages are that inflation may erode the value of your income (that lump sum might have been better invested in common stock, which offers some chance of keeping pace with inflation) and that you may die prematurely. It's possible to pay out $50,000 one year and be forced to join your ancestors the next, leaving the insurance company with a nice profit. If there is a heaven, which I doubt, there must be an awful lot of disgruntled angels who rue the day they ever heard of annuities. On the other hand, it's fun to beat the company to it. The prospect of making a profit on the deal does, you will agree, considerably increase the incentive to live to 120. (See also ENDOWMENT.)

APPRECIATION
An increase in the value of an asset. Property and stocks don't go up, they appreciate. There's no reason for this; it merely sounds more elegant. It's very much part of that

odd vocabulary which the stock exchange uses to enhance its respectability. Financial journalists often try to go still further. If you read the daily stock market report in the paper (or listen to it on the radio) you will see that there are a dozen or more ways of saying "up." Stocks may "harden," "edge higher," "strengthen," or "improve." This means, as a rule, that they have put on very little. I spent a year, long ago, writing part of the *Financial Times*'s report and I remember how hard we tried to think up new words. I mean, how many times can you say "edge higher" or "strengthen" in one paragraph? The temptation to resort to puns was irresistible. Motor shares invariably "accelerated" and cement shares "hardened." They still do.

ARBITRAGE
Buying and selling stocks, commodities, or currencies in different markets, taking advantage of different rates to make a profit. This is very much a game for the professional, because one has to be right on top of price movements. A brokerage house is much better placed than any individual, outside the market, to spot small differentials in a particular stock between, say, New York and San Francisco. The deal generally involves buying the stock in one place and simultaneously selling it short (see SELLING SHORT) at a slightly higher price in another.

ASSETS STRIPPING
Taking over a company and selling off — or stripping — most of its assets. These may be unwanted properties, machinery, or stocks of goods and raw materials. Firms tend to be more efficient in their use of assets than they were ten or

twenty years ago (the take-over boom has acted as a powerful spur) but the scope for stripping still seems to be considerable. It calls for a sharp eye, discretion, and the ability to make an utterly realistic assessment of what a firm's assets are worth. Many economists argue that the strippers are financial hyenas whose activities are of little help to the community: they throw people out of work and reduce competition. Others maintain that, by keeping potential victims on their toes, they perform a useful economic function. (See BALANCE SHEET.)

AUDITOR
A financial referee whose job it is to examine a company's books and confirm that its accounts give a "true and fair view" of its position. He may also be asked to inspect the records of nontrading organizations such as social clubs. Auditors are generally accountants appointed by the company's directors, who also fix their fee. And yet, they are in many ways the stockholders' champions. They are entitled to demand books, documents, and correspondence, and to insist on detailed explanations. If the directors have been up to no good, the auditor is supposed to qualify his report in a suitable manner.

The auditors' statement is always included in a company's annual report, and although it is usually printed in annoyingly small type, it's well worth an investor's while to read it. Auditors are independent accountants, and failure to point out misbehavior can lead to an action for professional negligence. But the temptation to close one's eyes may, occasionally, prove irresistible. And even if they are completely honest, there is always room for error because quite a lot has to be taken on trust. One of the main areas of company fraud, for example, is the valuation of stocks.

These consist, as a rule, of raw materials and finished or unfinished products, and may be substantial. It is clearly impossible for an auditor to check every single item, down to the last postage stamp, and to decide what the total may be worth at any given moment. He can satisfy himself that proper methods of assessment have been used, and make personal spot checks. But since valuation is, like the calculation of profit, more a matter of opinion than a strict fact, it is virtually impossible to insure 100 per cent accuracy.

Club accounts are usually simpler, and irregularities much easier to detect. It's surprising how many clubs fail to keep proper records, and how often an officer dips into the till. One well-known method of fraud, known as "teeming and lading," involves bar takings. The bar manager hands them to the treasurer once a month, and he is supposed to pay them into the bank. He may, however, delay doing so, and use the money to settle personal bills. This is not, of course, fraudulent in itself, but it's often the start of trouble. He may find himself unable, the following month, to make up the difference, or the temptation to repeat the exercise may be too strong. By the end of the financial year there's a considerable gap between the amount actually in the bank and the amount which should be there. Sometimes the treasurer can bridge the gap by borrowing; sometimes he decides to run off with the lot. The obvious answer is for club officials to cross-check each others' activities right through the year. Many people, though, feel this would be an insult to someone who, after all, gives his services for free. The possibility of fraud doesn't occur to them until it's too late.

AVERAGING

The 100 shares you've bought go down, right? You're still keen on them, so you buy another 100 at the lower level. You now hold 200 at an average price lower than the one you paid when you first took a fancy to this particular investment. That's called averaging. It means that the price doesn't have to go up by as much before you show a profit. The case for averaging is strongest when the shares are depressed by factors which are clearly temporary and have nothing to do with the shares' basic merit. They may, for example, suffer during one of those irrational bouts of jitters which affects all stock markets from time to time. But beware of overoptimism. Averaging makes sense only if your original judgment was correct. Wishful thinking merely makes the situation worse. Averaging up, rather than down, usually makes better financial sense because it goes with the trend, rather than against it.

BACKWARD-BENDING SUPPLY CURVE

There really is such a thing. It's a concept which holds that it is socially disadvantageous to pay wages above some indicated level because if one pays these higher wages the total output declines. The worker will find that he can supply his needs with fewer days of work and will simply lie down on the job. *Some* workers are like that, but as a generalization the backward-bending supply curve theory is full of holes. Indeed, it's a myth.

BAD BANKING MADE AMERICA GREAT

One of those slogans which become folklore through repetition. American banking did not really get under way until the country won its independence from Britain; the men who founded the new nation also started its first banks. The First Bank of the United States was established, by charter from Congress, in 1791. It was essentially a private bank, but the government was a part owner. The bank provided, among other things, a sound and stable currency and did a great deal of good. But the bank also had its opponents, including Jefferson, and when the charter expired in 1811 it was not renewed. The Second Bank of the United States was established in 1816 and operated successfully for several years before it, too, succumbed to opposition forces. These forces consisted chiefly of people who felt that state banks were more appropriate to the needs of local communities and that control over banking should be in the hands of state governments. Their victory ended, for a long period of time, the policy of regulating bank credit and the nation's currency through a federal bank.

The almost frantic expansion of state banks which followed marked the beginning of one of the most interesting periods in the whole history of banking. It has been called "a striking symbol of the American spirit of enterprise," and "an example of the kind of recklessness that gives banking a bad name." Take your pick. By today's standards, certainly, American banking of the nineteenth century seems astonishingly rash — and often downright crooked. But today's America is not the same as the America of the 1850s — a country with enormous potential, but populated by only a tenth of the present number and just beginning to feel the impact of the industrial revolution. The state banks were the chief source of badly needed credit and capital. If they exceeded the bounds of sound banking practice — well, so did everybody else.

In almost a century of "free banking" (meaning the more or less automatic granting of charters to anyone who could meet certain conditions) there were countless examples of fraud and plain incompetence. People could and did start new banks on very little capital and with only a scant knowledge of banking practice. Far more citizens lost money through bank failures than through bank robberies, later glamorized in Hollywood films. Booms frequently got out of hand and were followed by collapse and financial panic. But the banks were also a great driving force for economic growth and change. They grew up with the towns they served. The banker was as much a pioneer as the farmers and developers he helped. The typical small-town bank numbered its depositors in hundreds and had a staff of four or five people working in surroundings which were startlingly different from the plush premises most bankers like to have today. If the community prospered, so did the bank. If not, the banker was just as likely to find himself in trouble as his customers.

BAD DEBTS
An occupational hazard of business. Modern society cannot function without debt, and inevitably some of it goes bad. Restaurants and stores are frequent casualties, but anyone who extends credit to someone else is a potential victim.

The only way to avoid bad debts is to refuse to lend money or give credit. Most firms make a provision for bad and doubtful debts, but if they're wise they also recognize potential traps and take as much care as possible not to fall into them.

Banks, which are perhaps more vulnerable than anyone else, have a carefully worked out set of rules which, they believe, protects them as far as is humanly possible. They teach managers to avoid excessive lending on security values, to watch out for signs that customers are overextending themselves, to recognize overoptimistic balance sheets, to beware of people whose fortunes depend too much on one trade customer, and to spot glib characters who know every facet of fraud and don't hesitate to make use of it. But so much depends on personal judgment — one's assessment of another man's character, ability, integrity, and prospects — that there must always be room for error. There are, moreover, factors beyond a customer's control, including floods and natural disasters for farmers, and sudden death or illness. Many sickly accounts can be nursed back to health by careful handling at the right time: it's dangerous to throw good money after bad, but there are many occasions when a little understanding is the best form of protection. The avoidance of bad debts is not necessarily and completely a proof of business acumen. It may simply be a sign of excessive timidity. Each lender, whether businessman or banker, must make up his own mind about the people he deals with. If in spite of all care and prudence, he still finds himself faced with the danger of loss, the principles of recovery come into play. The law is on his side, but this may not be enough: one usually succeeds in recovering only part of the original loan or debt.

BALANCE OF PAYMENTS
An attempt to show the effects of financial transactions a country carries on with foreigners. Wrongly assumed to be a reliable barometer to economic health, the balance of payments is no guide to economic performance or productivity: a country can have a big payments surplus and a stagnant economy, as Britain did in 1971. Key factors affecting the balance of payments are imports and exports, earnings from sources like insurance and shipping, and movements of capital between one country and the rest of the world. The latter, in particular, can fluctuate quite sharply. Another big influence is the inflow and outflow of so-called hot money.

There is nothing sinful in a balance-of-payments deficit as such: if every country in the world tried to run a permanent surplus, international trade would dry up. But the ability to carry a sizable deficit for any period of time depends on the strength of other assets. If an individual owns a house, and assets like stocks that can be readily turned into cash, no one will worry if he runs up an overdraft. It's the same with a country. Britain has formidable overseas assets, in the form of investments in stocks and factories abroad, but most of these are privately owned and not readily available to the Government. It therefore has to rely chiefly on its "liquid assets" — gold and currency reserves (see GOLD). When these are low, foreigners tend to get worried about our ability to defend the existing exchange rate and withdraw their money. This happened under Mr. Wilson's government. Many economists feel that Mr. Wilson exaggerated the seriousness of the problem, and in so doing produced more trouble than necessary for both the Government and the country. They resent the fact that the payments deficit was presented as a vast political and moral issue, curable only if everyone worked twice as hard. The balance of payments, they say, is a pseudo problem, easily solved through greater exchange-rate flexibility. (See EXCHANGE CONTROL.)

BALANCE SHEET
A piece of paper which shows the financial position of a company at a specific date. On the left are liabilities, and these may include the following:

> **Issued share capital:** the money put up by stockholders. Since it is mostly permanent capital, there is no repayment date. It cannot be suddenly withdrawn.
>
> **Mortgages, debenture stock, loan capital:** this is borrowed money which may or may not have a definite repayment date.
>
> **Reserves:** these are profits which have been retained in the business, and therefore belong to stockholders. They may be revenue reserves (profits which originate from trading) or capital reserves (profits which arise from the sale of capital assets). It's largely a bookkeeping item, because the money is being employed in the business.
>
> **Current liabilities:** these include items which are liable to fluctuation, such as bank overdrafts, money owed to the tax man, and trade creditors.

Assets are on the right-hand side of the balance sheet, and include the following:

> **Fixed assets:** factories, machinery, transport, and other permanent fixtures, such as office property. They are employed for the purpose of running the business — not for resale. Most balance sheets show the cost and a recent valuation; the activity of take-over bidders has made most boards mindful of the need to show up-to-date values.

Good will: a nebulous term, basically meaning the value put upon the company's reputation. It may have been around for a long time and be highly regarded in its industry, or it may have acquired subsidiaries at a very favorable price. Because good will is such an intangible item, it tends to be the subject of considerable debate among financial purists. Some think it should be excluded altogether; all agree that it complicates investment analysis.

Current assets: these are the assets held by the company with the object of converting them into cash. The most important categories are debtors' balances (money due from customers), cash and near cash such as short-term loans and tax reserve certificates, and stocks and work in progress.

The surplus of current assets over current liabilities is known as the company's "working capital." It measures the extent to which the company can finance any increase in turnover. If working capital is nonexistent, watch out. It may be a sign of trouble.

Balance sheets are drawn up (the official word is "struck") on a certain date. For this reason, they are a record of the past, and should not be seen as a reliable guide to the future. They are usually several months old by the time they are published. Major items in them may be quite misleading: variables like stocks, creditors, and overdrafts may have changed considerably within a short period.

A balance sheet, moreover, does not always give a true picture even of the past. It shows how much money has been spent, but not whether it has been spent wisely. Fixed assets are a major item, and stock market analysts frequently stress the "assets backing" for a stock. But assets are only worth what they produce in terms of earnings. What use is a huge factory, entered at cost price, if it turns out goods which one can no longer sell at a profit? (See also ASSETS STRIPPING, DEBENTURES, and PROFIT.)

BANKRUPT

A person legally declared unable to pay his debts. The word is said to have originated in Renaissance Italy, at a time when bankers and moneychangers conducted their affairs from benches or stalls on the Italian bourse. When one failed or became insolvent, his bench was destroyed, and the name *banco-rotto*, or "broken bench," was given to him. To the French, the word became *banqueroute*; to the English, "banker out." In time it became "bankrupt."

A bankrupt used to be treated as an outcast, and bankruptcy still has a certain stigma attached to it. But the sting is not nearly as sharp as it used to be. It no longer strikes a bankrupt in Britain as much of a hardship, for example, to be prevented from voting in the House of Lords or House of Commons. And it's a mistake to think that a bankrupt automatically loses everything. Both Britain and America allow certain exemptions.

More and more, bankruptcy is regarded as an acceptable way out of deep financial trouble, a way of wiping the slate clean. It isn't pleasant, of course, but it's better than stealing or having a nervous breakdown. Some people even argue that bankruptcy was originally derived from the Bible. They quote from the Revised Standard Version: "At the end of every seven years you shall grant a release. And this is the manner of the release: every creditor shall release what he has lent to his neighbor; he shall not exact it of his neighbor, his brother, because the Lord's release has been proclaimed."

You can become a bankrupt by filing a petition with the court, or letting a creditor do so, together with a list of your assets and people to whom you owe money. In most cases the debtor has no assets and challenging him, in court, is not only a waste of time but tends to be expensive — since legal fees have to be paid.

You may apply for a discharge at any time after that, and whether you get it or not depends on whether the court thinks you have made sufficient effort to repay all or part of your debts.

Bankruptcy has increased tremendously in recent years, and one good reason is the comparative ease with which one can nowadays get credit. There have never been so many pressures on people to go in for installment buying, or to borrow money. The bigger the temptation, the greater the likelihood of financial disaster. Many well-known people have, over the last decade, filed a petition for bankruptcy, without finding themselves condemned as sinners. George Sanders, Betty Hutton, and Mickey Rooney all trooped through courts and survived. In the United States, people with large debts can opt for an alternative method of bankruptcy known as "Chapter XIII." Under this, the bankrupt doesn't seek release from what he owes, but asks for an extended period of time to pay what he owes — usually three years. Chapter XIII probably amounts to the most realistic approach to the whole problem.

The only time a bankrupt finds himself in really serious trouble is when someone can prove that fraud is involved. Example: knowing that his business is failing, a fraudulent trader may order goods to the maximum that his credit will stand — and then "give" them to a friend or relative or transfer them to a source from where he can recover them when he's ready to start up in business again. You'd be surprised how many people try this sort of thing and how few get away with it.

BASLE CLUB

One of Europe's most influential conclaves. Officially known as the Bank for International Settlements, it was conceived in the late 1920s as part of an attempt to "take finance out of politics." The bank was founded by leading European central banks, and is, essentially, a meeting ground of central bank governors.

Once a month, they get together in the Euler or Schweitzerhof Hotel for a weekend of informal talks, with just a perfunctory official session with other BIS officials. Politicians are neither invited nor welcome. The Basle Club has been described as "essentially a team of maintenance men, trying to keep the mechanism of the international monetary system humming smoothly." It is an apt description. They are the experts who know how the machinery works, but ultimately it's the politicians who make the key decisions. Central bankers usually try to get on with their political masters, but are very much aware that the need to win public favor may lead to departures from financial orthodoxy. They can recommend a certain course of action, but the final say lies with the finance ministers of each country. Not surprisingly, this situation often leads to friction. The most widely publicized clash of recent years was that between Mr. Harold Wilson and Lord Cromer, Governor of the Bank of England when Labour won power in 1964: when his Lordship's term was up the Government decided to replace him with someone they thought less hostile. Similar clashes have taken place in other countries, notably Germany and the United States. And yet, the Basle Club has often bailed out politicians when they appear to be in trouble. When Labour hit its first financial crisis, shortly after the 1964 election, Lord Cromer telephoned each of his fellow club members and within twenty-four hours put together a $3 billion loan. It was impressive proof of the club's ability to act quietly, and secretly, when the need arises.

More recently, the club has been an important forum for discussing such questions as sterling's role as a reserve currency, the future of gold, and greater exchange-rate flexibility. The so-called Basle Agreement resulted largely from its deliberations. No central banker can ignore the fact that politics plays a big part in the Capitalist Way of Finance — but the Basle Club, meeting so close to where the Gnomes of Zürich allegedly plot the downfall of the system, does its best to see that political fancy is turned into the bankers' idea of down-to-earth, realistic, matter-of-fact policy.

BEAR

Someone who sells stocks he doesn't own in the hope that he can buy them at a lower price before delivery is due. The term is also applied, generally, to those who take a pessimistic view of the future: they are said to be "bearish."

A bull is exactly the opposite — someone who buys shares in the hope of the price going up. And in the same way, to be "bullish" is to feel optimistic about the future.

A "bear market" is one which has seen a prolonged fall in prices, and which does not look capable of a sustained recovery.

A concerted attack by speculators is known as a "bear raid." People are selling a stock, or a currency, which they haven't got, hoping that the price will fall. They then move in, buy at the lower level, cover their commitment, and pocket the difference. A "bear squeeze" is exactly the opposite; prices are forced up, and the stock or currency which the bears need to clear their commitments are withheld, so that the bears have to pay heavily.

BEGGAR-MY-NEIGHBOR
Selfishness in trading partners; one country following restrictive policies at the expense of another. Governments are always tempted to protect themselves from foreign competition through high tariffs and other measures, and there have been periods when protectionism has been fashionable almost everywhere.

The astonishing growth in world trade over the past few decades owes much to a widespread awareness, among Western Industrial nations, that this sort of thing can backfire. If one country pulls down the shutters, there is nothing to stop the others from doing the same. Supranational institutions like the International Monetary Fund are pledged to fight for free trade, and the United States has been remarkably liberal since the last world war. In Britain, the refusal of the 1964–70 Labour Government to have anything to do with import quotas — putting a limit on the quantity of foreign goods allowed into the country — was chiefly due to fears of retaliation.

Nevertheless, protectionism is on the increase. The Americans, in particular, have become impatient — strong political pressure groups in Washington frequently stress that Japan's restrictive trade policies, and arrangements such as the EEC's Common Agricultural Policy, call for an effective answer. Any major move toward beggar-my-neighbor policies would be a blow for countries which depend on exports to keep their balance sheets straight. These include Britain — and, worse, most of the developing countries.

BEHAVIORAL SCIENCE
Attempts to find out not only what men do, but why they do it. Behavioral scientists are increasingly used by organiza-

tions to help with management problems — to identify talent, improve leadership, raise the level of communications, and reduce wastage of human effort. It's a worthy cause, because it recognizes that business success depends on more than facts and figures. Dozens of books have been published on the subject, especially in the United States, and most of them are well worth reading. Inevitably, though, behavioral scientists themselves are often so fascinated by the theoretical side of their studies that they move away from reality. And, of course, they have developed their own jargon: they talk of "self-actualization" (know yourself, and make the most of your talents) and "insightful management."

A London business school student, not long ago, injected a badly needed touch of humor into the whole matter by suggesting that the dramatic works of Shakespeare, commonly supposed to have been written simply for the theater, were in fact originally used as case studies in organizational behavior. In case No. 20 (*Romeo and Juliet*), "we see the harmful effects of a breakdown in communications between two organizations in an oligopolistic context. This situation is not rectified until informal inter-organizational communications have been set up at an employee level, with disastrous results." Case No. 26 (*Hamlet*), the student added, was about "a highly sophisticated young executive who was quite unable to make decisions at all." Shakespeare, clearly, was well ahead of his time; it's a pity that modern behavioral scientists can't write so entertainingly.

BIG BOARD
The popular term for the New York Stock Exchange, by far the largest and most influential stock market in the United States. The next largest market is the American Stock Exchange, popularly known as the "Amex," which specializes

in smaller up-and-coming companies. There are stock exchanges in many other cities, including Boston, Detroit, Cincinnati, and San Francisco, which make a market in local corporations, and in stocks already listed on the Big Board. There's also a huge and important over-the-counter market, which is not really a single market at all but a collection of dealers scattered all over the country.

BILL
The one thing no one seems to get around to freezing. It's also: a) the beak of a bird or anything like it, b) a concave battle ax with a long wooden handle, and c) a list of dishes. Few words, indeed, have a greater variety of meanings. In commerce and finance, "bill" is used in conjunction with dozens of other words or phrases. Perhaps the most popular is "bill of exchange," which is quite simply an order for the making of payment, used mainly in international trade. If you and I were doing business together, I'd issue a bill of exchange asking a bank, or some other party, to pay you a certain sum of money at a certain date. To be valid, the bank (or other party) would have to "accept" it by signing its/his name across the face of the bill. Once this is done (and providing the signature is of high standing) the bill is negotiable and may in fact change ownership several times during its life — usually three to six months.

BLACK FRIDAY
A phrase coined more than a hundred years ago, after several disastrous financial events happened on a Friday. Many people in the financial world — on both sides of the Atlantic — still believe that there is a jinx on that particular day of the week. In part, this is due to the fact that investors and others often develop preweekend nerves. Week-

ends have a habit of producing unpleasant news, and speculators often try to guard themselves against that possibility by getting out on Fridays. This, in turn, sometimes leads to sharp setbacks in the stock market — headlined, in the next day's newspapers, as BLACK FRIDAY.

I don't go along with the jinx theory. I have seen too much bad news break on other days of the week. And I have witnessed some absolutely splendid Fridays. "January," Mark Twain once wrote, "is a dangerous month for speculation. Other dangerous months are February, March, April, May, June . . ." Precisely.

BLUE CHIP
A high-quality common stock. The name comes, oddly enough, from a gambling chip — the highest valued chips are colored blue. Oddly, because blue chip stocks are regarded as the aristocrats of the market, and are not normally called a gamble. They have usually been favored by investors for many years and are established leaders. General Motors is a good example.

Blue chips are less risky than some of the more adventurous stocks, but it's a mistake to assume that, just because they have a fancy name, they are loss-proof. Their very success may be against them: they may have reached heights where dynamic growth is a thing of the past. (The market generally makes a distinction between old and new; the new blue chips include somewhat lively stocks like Xerox and IBM.) Timing, moreover, is just as important with blue chip stocks as with everything else. A market leader is more sensitive to adverse national news than many a small company. And there may be periods when investors' enthusiasm has run too far ahead of actual performance. If you buy at the wrong moment you may lose money, blue chip or not.

BLUE SKY LAWS

Popular name for laws enacted in various U.S. states to protect the public against security frauds. The term is thought to have originated when a judge ruled that a particular stock had about the same value "as a patch of blue sky." The laws apply mainly to the registration and sale of new securities, and tend to vary among different states.

BOARD MEETING

An event designed to make company directors feel important. Someone once said that a lot of board meetings are held each month for no better reason than that it's been a month since the last one. This isn't the whole story. A great many more are held because they impress the rest of the office, and because they save directors the embarrassment of having to make tricky decisions on their own. At every meeting there is at least one character who obviously hates the idea of returning to his desk. So he takes a molehill and expertly develops it into a mountain. He asks questions, raises points, requests additional data, demurs, and delays. He covers indefinite ideas with infinite words. And at the end of the meeting he suggests another one. Of course.

The passion for meetings is dangerous, as well as tiresome, because it frequently harms relationships which have been carefully built up over the years. You may lose your temper in the heat of debate, or alienate valuable allies by taking their opponents' side in a particular argument. You may commit frightful indiscretions, lose face, and even find yourself goaded into the ultimate folly — resignation. It all gets jotted down in "minutes": the chap who thought up that one had a sense of humor.

People with multiple directorships are sometimes so hard-pressed that they forget which company's board meeting they are at. One well-known property developer, Harry Jasper, held 400 directorships at the height of his career. One effective way of avoiding this kind of trap is to refuse ever to serve on a board. Another is to give your secretary explicit instructions on how to avoid getting you involved in meetings. The next time someone telephones to ask you to come to a meeting, get her to purr sweetly and say: "Sorry, he can't. He's in a meeting."

BOILER ROOM OPERATION
Wall Street jargon for efforts to sell stocks over the telephone. In a typical boiler room there are rows of desks with nothing but telephones on them. Each will be manned by a fast-talking salesman who will try to sell highly speculative stocks (in other words, stocks of questionable value) to overeager members of the public. The answer is simple: hang up. No matter how persuasive the voice at the other end, no matter how easy it sounds to make a quick killing, the gullible buyer will usually end up the loser. Some firms also offer bargain stocks by mail; millions of dollars are lost each year in this way.

BOND
An IOU issued by a government, local authority, or company as a promise to repay money over a period of time. People buy bonds to get the interest paid on them — the same way people put money in banks to get interest. Bonds with less than five years to run are usually called "short-dated"; those with a life of between ten and twenty years are medium; those with a life of more than twenty are long. Bonds may also be undated or irredeemable (in other words, not terminable by repayment) and some companies issue convertible bonds — meaning they can be converted

into a fixed number of shares of its common (or "ordinary") stock at some future date. The attraction of the "convertible" is that it offers the security of a fixed income, plus the chance of a profit if the common stock into which the bond is convertible should go up in market value.

BOONDOGGLE
Wasteful or uneconomic labor. It's one of the more colorful terms to come out of the depression which followed the Great Crash, a period in which government efforts to create employment sometimes resulted in useless or frivolous activity. Boondoggle still exists, but the term is not much used.

BORROWING BIG
According to Aristotle Onassis, one of the surest ways to success. It's often easier to borrow half a million dollars than ten thousand, *providing* you have the right sort of proposition and can convince the lender that you can make it work. The timid office worker, confronting his bank manager with a modest request, will never make large profits for the bank. The self-confident entrepreneur with bold ideas, on the other hand, could be a potential millionaire. And once the lender has decided to back you, he has a vested interest to insure your success. Other Onassis ingredients: "keep looking tanned, live in an elegant building — even if you're in the cellar — and be seen in smart restaurants, even if you nurse one drink."

I'm not sure about the tan. It's a status symbol of sorts, a sign that you are doing well. But some people (notably bankers) may also take it as proof that you are excessively fond of the frivolous pursuit of pleasure. I can see why one should live in an elegant building: the right address still carries a lot of weight. And I suppose if you patronize smart restaurants there's always a chance that you will make the acquaintance of someone like Mr. Onassis — which could speed things up quite a bit. But I suspect Mr. Onassis is holding out on us. The con game he describes is far from foolproof: I know too many people who can (and do) play it to perfection without making any significant progress.

BOYCOTT

When General de Gaulle first mounted his attack on the dollar, many Americans stopped drinking French wine and eating Camembert. That was a boycott. When Rhodesia, a British colony, decided to break away from Britain, the Government in London announced a ban on trade between the two countries. They called this ban "sanctions," but it was a boycott.

The word comes from Captain C. C. Boycott, an English land agent with whom the Irish refused to deal in the land-tenure disturbances of 1879–1881. Boycotting can take many different forms. Idealists in Britain have, for many years, refused to eat South African oranges in protest against that country's racial policies, and labor unions sometimes urge a boycott of some company's products because the management refuses to allow union organization. Manufacturers occasionally boycott, or black-list, a retailer in order to enforce restrictions on competition.

To succeed it must be difficult, if not impossible, for the other side to turn elsewhere. The French were not unduly worried about the boycott on Camembert because the boycott was by no means universal in America itself. Even the boycott against Rhodesia, although fully supported by the United Nations, has not been fully effective because South Africa, Portugal, and others have been more than ready to bridge the gap. The best chance of success obviously lies in situations where small firms, making a specialized product, are boycotted by their regular customers or where a well-organized labor union refuses to handle goods supplied by a firm where a labor dispute is taking place. The motives are not always clear-cut, and may sometimes be not only objectionable but sinister.

BRETTON WOODS

A town in New Hampshire, where forty-four nations decided, in July 1944, to set up a new international monetary system. The previous system had been based on the so-called gold standard, but it collapsed in the 1930s. The confusion and growth in nationalistic policies which followed highlighted the need for an entirely new system. Plans had been drawn up some time before, and the Bretton Woods Conference was called to discuss details. Among the delegations were representatives of most of the Allies, including the Soviet Union and other East European countries; nations of the British Empire; and western European and Latin American countries. Many of them were unhappy with Anglo-American domination of the conference, and the Soviet Union announced that it would not take part in the new system.

British economist John Maynard Keynes, one of the key figures at the conference, suggested the creation of an international bank, which could grant credits to its members. The credits, in the form of a new international currency called the *bancor,* would be given to nations on the basis of their prewar share of world trade. America vetoed the idea (chiefly because Britain stood to gain more than the United States) but agreement was reached on the creation of two new institutions. One, the World Bank, was intended to provide loans to developing nations and to countries whose economies had been severely damaged by the war. The other, known as the International Monetary Fund, was given responsibility for supervising the system. (See also INTERNATIONAL MONETARY FUND and WORLD BANK.)

BUCKET SHOP
Slang term for a dealer in stocks, not a member of the stock exchange, who accepts your order and your money to buy in the market — but doesn't execute the order. Instead he pockets the money and gambles on his ability to buy the stock you want at a lower price and make a profit for himself on the order. His activities are illegal and are nowadays practically nonexistent. (See also BOILER ROOM OPERATION.)

BUDGET
In business, an attempt to lay down a blueprint for future operations. The system varies from firm to firm, but it is common for the directors to devise a master budget, and to ask each department to provide one of its own. Departmental heads try to predict their probable income and expenditure during the coming year, and submit their budgets to the board. Forecasts, alas, often go wrong and in a well-run company regular comparisons are made between budgeted results and actual achievement. Minor deviations don't really count, but any major gap ought to lead to a thorough reappraisal. A common fault is overoptimism about sales, and an underestimate of costs. The remedy is swift realistic action but it's surprising how often the top management decides to condone, or even to endorse, what has clearly turned out to be a piece of wishful thinking.

BUFFER STOCKS

A scheme designed to iron out fluctuations in the price of raw materials, or to insure continuity of supply. Bad weather, disease, or some other adverse factor may, for example, substantially reduce production of rubber, cotton, or tea in a particular year. The normal market response would be for prices to rise sharply. (In practice, alternative sources of supply are often available.) A buffer stock scheme would help to prevent this. It may be operated by the government or by the industry itself, and it involves building up a stockpile of raw materials which can be used, when necessary, to bridge the gap.

As a rule, the people operating such a scheme fix a "ceiling" and a "floor" price. When prices reach the ceiling, the operators sell from their stockpile. When prices drop to the floor, they buy the raw material (or "primary product," as some experts insist on calling it) and add it to the hoard. It's much the same method as that normally applied in currency markets, where stocks of gold and foreign paper money are used to keep exchange rates within certain defined limits. It sounds fine in theory, and has been successfully used to prevent unwanted booms and slumps. But it clearly works only in the case of materials which can be stored at relatively little cost. The creation of an artificial market, too, may have unfortunate long-term effects. It is certainly open to abuse: buffer stocks tend to be operated more in the interests of producers than consumers.

BULL

Conventional dictionaries include the following definitions: the male of a bovine animal, and of a whale, walrus, elephant, or moose; policeman; humbug; statement made ludicrous by some inconsistency or contradiction which it contains; an edict by the Pope.

Don't ever let anyone hear you use any of them around Wall Street. In the money world, a bull is a speculator who takes an optimistic view of the future price of stocks in general or a specific stock. The term is often extended beyond stocks to the economy, the state of trade in a particular area, or individual organizations. An optimistic outlook is said to be "bullish," meaning hopeful.

A bull *may* be a humbug and may even behave, on occasions, like an elephant. But on the whole, he tends to be a cheerful, likable sort of fellow. (See also BEAR.)

BUSINESS CONFIDENCE

The general state of opinion among businessmen at any given time. Said to be "a tender plant," easily damaged if a politician says the wrong word. Actually, it depends on a great many factors — the state of world trade, the prospects for economic growth at home, the availability of credit, the willingness (and ability) of customers to place new orders and pay for those already executed, the views of friends and colleagues, and the amount of dry martini inside a businessman at the precise moment when he is asked for his opinion.

Various organizations attempt to measure business confidence from time to time, but the result is almost invariably unreliable. This is partly because confidence varies from industry to industry, and from firm to firm. The chief reason, however, is that so many people lie. Their answer may be influenced by dislike of whatever government is in power, or by their eagerness to blame "general conditions" for their own lack of success. The average company report reads something like this: "The government has got the country into a terrible mess, industry is fed up and depressed, there is no incentive to do anything, prospects are bleak — *and our profits this year are forty per cent up.*"

Some businessmen think it's good policy to sound optimistic; optimism is infectious. Others think it's better not to let the other fellow know that you are doing well. If he is a customer, he might insist that you bring prices down. If he's a business contact or a supplier in trouble, he might try to get a loan. All such embarrassment can be avoided by the simple device of telling your hard-luck story before the other fellow gets a chance to do so. In America, not long ago, three Lebanese brothers became famous as "the crying Adjimmis" because they carried this to its obvious conclusion. They bought shoddy, dirt-cheap goods, advertised a "closing-down sale," and howled like a force-nine gale about the cruel fate which was compelling them to put "expensive quality goods" on the market at bargain prices.

Businessmen who run large corporations, with a quote on the stock market, will tell you that it's usually best to err on the side of caution in one's assessment of prospects. If you make an optimistic forecast, stockholders won't thank you, a year later, if it proves to have been justified. They are, after all, merely getting what you led them to expect. And God help you if things go wrong! A cautious forecast, on the other hand, gives you a good chance of being hailed as a hero if profits turn out to be better than expected. It will all be attributed to the excellence of management; governments only collect blame, not credit.

The most dismal people I know are shipowners. A few years ago I found myself on a luxury yacht, sailing toward Athens. My hosts were members of two of the wealthiest Greek shipping families. We drank gallons of Dom Perignon at breakfast and nibbled whitebait served by white-jacketed flunkies. At noon we switched to caviar and Château Lafite. This, I said, is the life. While we were eating, we discussed business. My hosts seemed deeply depressed. Shipping, they confided, was in a frightful state. Everyone was losing pots of money. Prospects were grim. Guiltily, I spent a whole three seconds toying with the idea of saying, No, thank you, I won't have another portion of caviar. Then I remembered what one of their fraternity, Basil Mavroleon, had told me years before: "Shipowners are always complaining. And when they die they leave a fortune."

BUSINESS CYCLE
Also called "trade cycle." It means alternating periods of ups and downs in business activity. Economists hold that the cycle is a continually recurring phenomenon of any business order, divided into characteristic phases. A typical cycle is made up of a period of expansion, a downturn or recession, a period of contraction, and an upturn or revival. The whole process used to last between five to ten years, but since the last world war cycles have been considerably shorter. The subject is highly complex: all sections do not turn up and down at the same time, and no two cycles are ever identical. There is no shortage of schemes for reducing swings in the economy, and governments spend much time and energy trying to smooth out ups and downs. The cycle has lost much of its old terror — but it certainly has not disappeared altogether.

BUSTED BONDS
Loans to foreign governments who have stopped paying interest due on them, and in many cases have failed to honor their commitment to repay the issue at a later date. This is a highly specialized market and one in which the speculative element predominates. Some are issues of South Amer-

ican states and cities which are partially or entirely in default, and others are bonds issued many years ago by countries now under communist control. Pre-Revolution Russian government bonds are well to the fore, along with Hungarian, Rumanian, and Baltic bonds. From time to time, some or all of these enjoy a revival of interest. It is usually sparked off by news of some move toward rapprochement between the communist and capitalist worlds; there is always someone ready to believe that in order to gain some trade advantage the communists will be willing to settle debts incurred by people they threw out of office several decades ago. The revival usually tends to be short-lived. Many busted bonds are also known as "lampshade bonds," because they do tend to make rather pretty lampshades!

BUY AMERICAN
Allegedly a fine way to demonstrate your love for your country. Foreigners take a less charitable view of it: to them it amounts to open protectionism and calls for retaliation. In Britain, Buy British campaigns tend to be launched whenever the pound is in trouble. The idea is to narrow the trade gap, and therefore help the balance of payments, by buying fewer foreign goods.

In 1968 a Czechoslovakian-born British M.P., Mr. Robert Maxwell, ran a Buy British campaign following an attempt by five Surbiton typists to demonstrate their patriotic fervor by working half an hour extra every day for free. Mr. Maxwell argued that buying British made more sense. Retailers cooperated by clearly marking certain goods with the Union Jack. The campaign was popular for a time, because it made ordinary people feel that they could do something to help. It inspired a whole range of other ideas, most of them dotty. One man wanted people to collect "useless gold trinkets" — old wedding rings, watches, and gold teeth — and take them to a specially created government purchasing center. Another, the managing director of a small company, persuaded his staff to pay overtime earnings into a national fund, out of which was to be financed the conversion of an "old obsolete aircraft carrier which has been lying moored up unused for 20 years into a floating overseas exhibition for Britain." Many people sent checks and money orders to the treasury. The whole thing petered out after a few weeks, as it deserved to do.

BUYERS' MARKET
See SELLERS' MARKET.

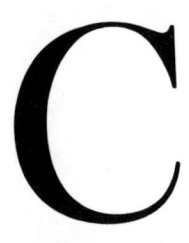

C

CAPITAL
Can be any asset which earns money, or which could be sold on the open market. If you own a house, that's capital. If you run a business, stocks of raw material or half-finished products may be capital. But it is usual to draw a distinction between assets that you cannot easily dispose of and those that are readily available. The excess of current assets

over current liabilities is known as one's working capital.

It's amazing how much difference a little capital can make to a young man's career. It allows him to choose between wage slavery and independence, gives him self-confidence, and widens his horizon. The sum does not have to be very large. Hundreds of prosperous companies were started on modest army gratuities after the Second World War. And many young men who left the parental nest with a business "dowry" have quickly achieved fame and fortune. If I were a millionaire, I reckon I could get both satisfaction and profit from backing able and ambitious young men — and taking a share stake in return. Alas, I'm still a little short of my first million. About $950,000 short, at a rough guess.

I'd rather not say anything about my working capital.

CAPITAL GAINS TAX

A tax on profit as distinct from income — "profit" meaning, in this case, any realized increase in the value of an asset — stocks, or a painting, or a diamond.

Short-term capital gains — profits from investments held less than six months — are treated just like ordinary income. You add your short-term profits to your salary income and pay taxes on the lot. Long-term capital gains — profits from investments held six months or longer — are treated the same way, except that half of them escape tax-free. In effect, long-term gains are taxed at half your normal rate (or 25 per cent, whichever is less). Gains over $50,000 a year are subject to a slightly higher maximum rate — but if you make that kind of profit you ought not to worry too much about taxes! (See also TAX-LOSS SELLING.)

CAPITAL INVESTMENT

Investment in new plant and machinery and one of the key factors in economic growth. It's modern equipment, more than an extra hour's hard work by individuals, that makes a country progress. In Germany, after the Second World War, businessmen had to buy new plant and machinery because the old lot was destroyed by Allied bombs and guns. In Japan, industrialists learned from the Americans that modern equipment is the surest way to high productivity and fast economic growth. In Britain, we made do with old plant and machinery because it was there, because it was intact, and because labor unions were suspicious of anything that looked like change. We might have got away from this but for the fact that constant financial crises prevented fast economic growth and forced companies to rely on outdated but undamaged equipment. The idea climate for investment is a booming, rapidly growing economy. Strong demand presses upon physical capacity, and makes firms want to expand. High profits give them the means to do so and are a much more important factor than allowances or grants.

CASH FLOW

.... want to have a conversation with accountants. Take cash in hand at the beginning of a year, add to it the profit you've made less tax and dividends paid, add depreciation (which is a cost, but not an outlay, and therefore available for a company's use), and, for good measure, whatever funds you've managed to raise during the year. There you have your "cash flow." It's a way of measuring what cash has gone through your fingers, but of course any proper measurement has to take

note of the use you've made of it. Accountants like to make a distinction between funds applied in everyday business and those used to buy permanent assets. When they talk of the latter, they like to use the phrase "discounted cash flow." It's really an attempt to put a value today on a flow of income in future years: in short, to assess the value of what we British call "jam tomorrow." If, for example, you buy another company, you take the cost of your purchase, less tax and investment allowances, and estimate the profit (less tax) it will give you over the period of its life. The trouble with this kind of exercise, of course, is that things seldom remain the same. Accountants accept this, but argue that it beats relying on pure guesswork.

CEMETERY CARE INVESTMENT FUND
One of the many specialized mutual funds catering for a professional group — in this case cemetery owners — or for some particular hang-up. There are funds for doctors, airline pilots, farmers, teachers, and people who don't like liquor, tobacco, drugs, munitions, and foreign securities. There's even a fund which invests almost exclusively under water.

These funds may all be sound (I cast no aspersions) but I personally tend to be wary of funds with a narrow range. It's a good sales gimmick, but the whole point of mutual fund investment is to spread one's risk and I don't think professional managers should impose rigid limits. It may mean that, in order to grow, they will have to choose stocks simply because they belong to a particular industry or trade, rather than on merit.

Don't look at the label; look at the record.

CHARACTER TEST

Every senior executive's idea of jolly, sadistic fun. The basic principle is simple: you lure people into embarrassing situations to see how they make out. The late Lord Beaverbrook — this is a true story — once invited a financial editor (who shall be nameless) to go on a trip to Canada with him. During a long train journey, he initiated the kind of drinking contest which, given the old man's skill with bottle and glass, no one could hope to beat him at. After four hours of solid imbibing, the poor chap was in a complete stupor. Beaverbrook rose without a word, staggered to his compartment, and fell asleep. The next morning the lord's wrath was awesome to behold: the financial editor, utterly bewildered, was dispatched home to England, and thereafter Beaverbrook always scornfully referred to him as "the man who gets drunk on trains." Stalin, Nikita Khrushchev tells us, had a similar urge to set up situations which allowed people to make fools of themselves. A little prodding here and there, a show of phony camaraderie, and another promising career was at an end.

The most dangerous time is the Christmas party season. Employers hold parties not, as is commonly supposed, to reward their staff for a good year's work, but to see how well they can hold their liquor. The widely held view that Christmas is the season of good will is a myth: it is, more than anything else, the season in which skillful operators identify and eventually eliminate their victims. An astonishingly large number of people, misled by the smile on the face of the office tiger and by the deliberately engineered atmosphere of conviviality, discard the caution they have displayed all year and walk straight into the trap. They burst into song, tell doubtful jokes, boast, drop the wrong names, and try to bully the managing director into joining them in a tap dance. They proposition the boss's secretary (refusing to take no for an answer) and encourage their own to move on to a chummy first-name basis — a gesture which destroys, for good, the relationship that ought to exist between a man and his daytime helpmate.

Above all, people say things to superiors, and even to rivals, which ought to remain unsaid. They confide to the boss, amid such merriment, that his staff call him "baggy-pants" and see him as a man with a soft heart, and a head to match. They score off a rival (or imagine they do) by putting him down in front of a couple of silly, but pretty, office girls. They embarrass a close colleague by giving everyone details of his private life. And they try to look big by making disparaging remarks about the chairman — remarks which, of course, are immediately reported back to him. A whole year's climbing may, in this way, be set back by an extra Scotch or martini. The wisest approach to an office party is to work out a strategy in advance: put down all the things you want to say, the things you know are guaranteed to impress. Drink only tonic water; you can switch to stronger stuff *at home* later on. Be relaxed, but in complete control. Don't say a word more than you planned to say. Remember that, when another executive pats you on the back, he is merely calculating where to stick the knife.

CHARTISM
See HEAD AND SHOULDERS.

CHEAP MONEY
Money available at a low rate of interest. Governments often use it to stimulate a flagging economy: cheap and easy credit is reckoned to be every bit as effective as tax cuts.

Some also see it as a means of securing social justice. People, they reason, should be able to buy, say, a home of their own without paying an exorbitant price for it. Bankers, inevitably, take a more cautious view. The Federal Reserve System ("the Fed") reckons, with good cause, that cheap money increases the inflationary pressures which have proved to be such a big problem in recent years. It also reckons that, by and large, politicians do not exercise enough restraint in public spending, and sees high interest rates as one of the few ways in which it can effectively impose some discipline. The era of really cheap money — at 2 per cent or so — may well be gone for good.

CLOSED-END FUNDS

Older, generally more solid relatives of mutual funds. Like mutual funds, they are in the business of investing other people's money. Unlike them, they have a fixed number of shares outstanding and they neither issue new shares nor buy back old ones: that's why they're called closed-ends. The various stock exchanges provide a market in their shares in the same way as any other company. You pay a stockbroker's fee to buy them, and the price is determined by the marketplace.

Closed-end funds tend to pay low incomes, but if they do well they may also hand out capital gains tax dividends — special payments from gains taken on some of their investments. These are usually described as nonrecurring, so it is obviously wise not to count on them when you first decide whether to buy. Another attraction, for many people, is that closed-ends often sell at less than the net value of their assets. But this may simply reflect the fact that market professionals don't think very much of their portfolio of stocks. And it isn't a lot of use unless the fund is about to be liquidated, meaning that its assets are being converted into cash. Given good management, closed-end funds can be a very profitable investment. Be sure, though, that you know what you're getting yourself into.

COGNITIVE PROCESS

Getting an idea. Some people are better at this than others, but they are not necessarily more successful. It's not just that the ideas men lose money — which they often do. People distrust men with ideas: they're considered dangerously overambitious. There are well-established rituals for disposing of ideas, and you should be familiar with at least some of them. Perhaps the most obvious is to give ten reasons why the idea won't work. This can be very effective, but generally means one has to know the subject very well. If you don't, and have no wish to expose your ignorance, it is better to treat the whole thing as a joke. You look at the proposer in astonishment and say: "You aren't serious about that, surely?" Another gambit is to hint that the idea, or at least something very much like it, has been tried before. But the most effective method, especially if there are accountants present, is to suggest that the cost of implementing it would be enormous. If this doesn't work you can always propose that it should be turned over to a committee — the corporate equivalent of a medieval death warrant. By the time the committee has finished, the fellow who had the audacity to start the whole thing will be loudest in denouncing it.

It is, of course, possible that you are one of those troublemakers who actually produce ideas. Must you? Well, perhaps you can't help yourself. I can offer only one suggestion, which has worked in my own case. Find a way of letting the boss think the idea is his; if he bites, you've made it. It is, of course, galling to see someone else get the credit, but such feelings are immature and unworthy of an executive.

COMAKER
Someone who has sufficient faith in you to take equal responsibility for settling a loan if you should fail to do so. Lenders like to have collateral, meaning something in addition to your solemn promise to repay. This can take the form of property, stocks, or jewels. But they may also settle for a guarantee from a friend who enjoys the required financial standing. Friends like that are not always easy to find; a lot of people believe in the old British dictum that "a friend in need is a bloody nuisance." Well you can't really blame them, can you?

COMMON AGRICULTURAL POLICY
A highly controversial scheme devised by the Common Market countries to protect their farmers. Or, as its creators once put it, "a bargain between German industry and French agriculture." Germany was the biggest food-importing country; France the biggest surplus producer. The deal seemed a natural. But the balance of advantages did not work out in Germany's favor, and the Germans became increasingly critical. The Common Agricultural Policy has been under attack for years, and was held to be one of the main arguments against Britain's entry into the EEC in 1962. Individual countries, including Britain, have long tried to protect their farmers in some way, and the CAP is merely an attempt to provide a common framework, with subsidies made available from a fund to which everyone contributes. But its blatant protectionism is resented in the

outside world, and it has plenty of opponents in the EEC itself. The planners have never fully succeeded in coping with one basic fact: Europe produces too much food.

COMMON MARKET
A commercial arrangement frequently (and erroneously) referred to as "Europe." Created in 1958, it aimed at abolishing trade barriers between member countries — and, eventually, at economic integration leading to the long-term goal of political unity. The first aim was achieved within ten years or so, but the others have been much more difficult to accomplish. There is a so-called European parliament, and there is no shortage of European organizations. Indeed, the casual visitor from the United States might be forgiven for concluding that supranational Europe already exists. But parliaments, councils, committees, and other setups are a front: they disguise the fact that there is no such thing as a genuine "European Community."

The European parliament lacks real power; important decisions are still taken at the national level, as they have always been. When Britain negotiated its own entry in 1971, the Government took great care to stress that no one nation could override another. Britain was keeping her own parliament, courts, and authorities. The English and Scottish legal systems would continue as before. And the "Community" does not cover defense policies.

Common Market enthusiasts still talk about political unity, but admit that progress is likely to be slow. Even in the commercial field, where the advantages of joining forces appeared most obvious, fact remains far removed from fancy. There is still no European company law, no common currency, no freedom from exchange control. The "American challenge" has not yet produced the kind of regrouping Jean-Jacques Schreiber, among others, considers so essential. Europe's opinion on Vietnam or Pakistan continues to carry little weight in Washington and Peking, and "European unity" has not been able to prevent outrageous events right on Europe's doorstep, such as the invasion of Czechoslovakia.

History, tradition, and different languages are, of course, the biggest obstacles. But part of the fault must lie with Europe's political leaders. Their visions of Europe have not produced any sense of personal involvement; the young, particularly, regard Brussels as little more than a bureaucratic paradise. Perhaps that will change one day, but it may take an awfully long time. (See also TREATY OF ROME.)

COMMON STOCK
So called because it is just that, the most common form of investment. In Britain, the words "ordinary" or "equity" are more generally used. Common or ordinary stock is issued by a company at a certain price to the public, thus offering ownership of the business to many people. Stockholders get to vote in the firm's affairs (one share, one vote) and are entitled to a share of its profits. In theory, they are the bosses. In practice, the small holder tends to have little or no say, except perhaps in dramatic situations like a takeover battle. With corporations getting larger all the time, it is difficult — and expensive — for an individual to mount an effective opposition to the management board. The board will pay lip service to him, but politely ignore his arguments. Only the biggest — or, occasionally, the most stubborn — holder commands any real respect. (See also ANNUAL GENERAL MEETING.)

COMPANY DOCTOR

An expert sent to save a business, if he can. His title is not an official one: it was bestowed by the financial press because it seemed appropriate. The company doctor is likely to be an accountant, a lawyer, or a management consultant. Occasionally, he is all three. His chief characteristic is an impersonal regard for facts — and the professional ability to assess them. Like any other doctor, he makes his diagnosis, suggests a cure, and helps to nurse a company through its difficulties. His desk-side manner is often blunt and abrupt. Company doctors are seldom popular. And few of them are rich. Comfortably off, yes. In the millionaire class, no.

A doctor, someone once said, is a chap who tells you that if you don't cut something out, he will. It's a message lots of businessmen would do well to remember.

COMPANY MEETING

See ANNUAL GENERAL MEETING.

COMPANY PLANE

See CORPORATE JET.

COMPANY TOWN

A community made up chiefly of the employees of one large business organization, which controls most of its activities. Company towns are especially prominent in Japan. I once spent a week in Hitachi City, a community in which almost everything — including the town hospital and fire station — is owned and operated by Hitachi. The company claims that, as a result, employees are looked after much better than they would be in a more normal town. This may be true, but there are several obvious drawbacks. One is that a company town's prosperity depends too much on one firm or industry; another is that, with all the policies dictated by the board of directors, there is generally little room for individual freedom. In America, Detroit comes close to being a company town, and I suppose the trend toward bigger and bigger units will produce more communities like this elsewhere. I'm glad I don't have to live in one. (See also PATERNALISM.)

COMPETITIVE SURVEILLANCE
A management catch phrase, coined by a group of Boston consultants. It's long and it scans well; you can quite safely use it at cocktail parties, and the person you are trying to impress won't have the slightest idea what it means. So what does it mean? It means finding out what the other man's doing. It means reading the papers, dissecting his annual report, stripping down and analyzing his latest products, and knowing when his top scientist is weary of his job and wants to move. It could also mean, although the Boston consulting group doesn't say so, industrial espionage. "Early intelligence," the group assures us, "opens a wide range of tactical options — in pricing, marketing and brinkmanship." And the payoff "can be very great indeed when properly related to the corporate strategy."

CONDOMINIUM
Another one of those fancy Latin words lawyers are so fond of. A condominium gives you a legal title to an apartment and an interest in the land and all improvements, which you hold in common with the other apartment owners.

Like a home or cooperative apartment owner, you can deduct mortgage interest and taxes paid on your income tax return. But unlike a cooperative owner, you are usually free to sell or lease at any price to anyone. Tax concessions apart, a condominium is a reasonable hedge against inflation and, therefore, beats renting. And chores such as trimming hedges and cleaning walks are taken care of by someone else. But that name! Imagine telling someone that you live in a condominium community. It sounds like a stockade.

CONFERENCE
Also known as a "convention." An essential feature of the twentieth-century way of life, for several reasons. One is that conferences keep many large, ugly, old-fashioned, uncomfortable hotels from going out of business. Another is that they satisfy the present-day craving for togetherness. They are a natural extension of committee meetings and annual dinners. They make people feel at home, real, important. Convention Man is not simply an individual, plagued by self-doubts. He is part of an important club, a forum which allows a group of people with some common interest to present a united front against the rest. Conventions confer status on those who attend them, and on the bodies which hold them. An organization that can afford to hold a national convention once a year clearly deserves to be taken seriously.

The chief products of conventions are speeches and resolutions. Occasionally, they also produce good ideas, but this is not the purpose of a convention. Newcomers sometimes make the mistake of thinking that they ought to air original thoughts, but they soon learn that this is an unwelcome approach. Such behavior challenges the spirit of togetherness, the carefully cultivated impression that everyone is in the same boat, rowing for the common good. Convention Man, at his best, is a master of the art of disseminating platitudes. The audience invariably gives him a standing ovation. In contrast, the fellow who tries to be different will usually find himself sitting down amid deafening silence. "What," one member of the audience will whisper to another, "was this damn fool talking about?"

CONFRONTATION
A discussion between opposed parties who sit in separate rooms and communicate through an intermediary. One of the words favored by newspaper headline writers, because it helps to dramatize particular situations. It's important, if you want to keep a sense of perspective, to familiarize yourself with some of the other headline terms.

Crackdown: any feeble attempt of authority to stand up to the truculence of a minority.

Tough Bargaining: a negotiating session in which management takes a little longer than usual to give in.

Backlash: a state of dismay and impotent muttering among groups who feel they are being picked on, but who don't really see what they can do about it.

Crisis: a flat point in a long-drawn-out, tedious dispute.

Tense Situation: a situation.

Grave Development: a development.

Prospects Are Bleak/Grim/Rosy: prospects are the same as any other day.

Victory: any more or less successful exaction of a wage award.

Shock: a predictable event likely to be received by the public with apathetic acquiescence. For example: "Fares Rise Shock," "Tax Rise Shock."

Lashes: criticizes.
Slams: a milder version of "lashes."
Flays: criticizes, with strong rhetorical touches, e.g. "Nader Flays Nixon."
Of Nationwide Concern: of arguable concern within a couple of miles of Wall Street.
Threat to Democracy: threat to the press.
Unfair Competition: competition.

CONGLOMERATE:

Take a firm making paper tissues, another importing wine, a third specializing in burglar alarms, and a fourth publishing classics. Put them all together under one roof and you've got a conglomerate. Or, if you like, a dog's breakfast. Basically, a conglomerate is a multipurpose, multi-industry company noted for hodgepodge acquisitions — an enterprise dedicated to proving that oil and water *do* mix.

An essential feature is common financial control and strong central management. From the investor's point of view the idea has considerable appeal, since it appears to give him a wide spread of interests. Unfortunately, performance does not always match up to promise. Purchases which seemed bargains frequently turn out to be duds the moment they are really put to the test. Picking companies in industries which one knows little or nothing about can be a dangerous business.

There is no shortage of cases, on both sides of the Atlantic, in which overoptimism has produced serious problems. For a time, all seems well. Take-over bids come so fast that all a stockholder can see is rising profits. If a conglomerate makes a bad buy, the fact is usually hidden by its accounting methods. The profits of the loss-making company are simply added to that of the parent, so that the overall profit still looks reasonable. The hope, naturally, is that good management can quickly achieve a dramatic improvement in the newcomer's figures. But more often than not, this improvement takes an awfully long time to materialize. This may be partly because the company's situation is more serious than the bidder had allowed for, and partly because his managerial talent has been spread over too many different companies. A big organization, with a wide range of interests, obviously has a better chance of overcoming this kind of snag than a smaller one. But even a giant can quickly lose its glamour if it has accumulated a large debt structure. Its stock market image is based on rapid profits growth, not on consolidation. If it runs out of steam, investors lose their enthusiasm. This, in turn, forces the conglomerate to stop bidding. If it stops bidding, it stops growing.

Conglomerates (the word comes from the Latin *conglomerare*, meaning "to roll together") enjoyed great popularity on Wall Street in the sixties, but are no longer in vogue. Analysts increasingly questioned the validity of profits and sales figures, and warned against overspeculation. Washington, too, found it too much and decided to curb the conglomerates' activities.

CONSTANT PRICES

One of the things which annoys economists is that nothing ever seems to stay the same. This is certainly true of prices, and it makes comparisons with the past not only difficult, but often quite misleading. So for the purpose of theorizing, economists like to assume that prices have stayed constant. You will sometimes see phrases like "at 1936 prices" or "at 1958 prices." Don't be fooled; there is, of course, no such thing. It's simply a splendid way of playing about with figures, and it's a game all can join.

CONSUMER DURABLE
A real favorite with economists, this; it means, roughly translated, "goods which last for a period of time," such as furniture, cars, houses, and washing machines. Food and drink are obviously in a different category, and their link with the word "consumption" is more obvious. Economists, though, persist in the notion that furniture and cars, too, are "consumed" rather than used. They say it's a more precise term; "consumed" implies that even durables wear out and have to be replaced; "used" has no such implication. They have a point, but don't apologize if the whole thing strikes you as a bit odd — you're not alone.

CONSUMER PRICE INDEX
An official attempt to measure price changes throughout the whole field of goods and services over which household expenditure is distributed. It covers wholesale prices and the prices paid by consumers for food, housing, fuel, furniture, clothing, transport, and medical care. Altogether, more than four hundred items go into the index, which is generally regarded as the most important pointer to the cost of living. Many labor unions have negotiated contracts which provide for periodic adjustments in wages linked to the changes reported in the index: these are known as "cost-of-living adjustments."

CONSUMER SOCIETY
A world obsessed with the symbols of material welfare — cars, washing machines, TV sets. A lot of experts on both sides of the Atlantic hold it responsible for social evils like violence and drug-taking. Their main target is the advertising industry, which, it is said, forces people to buy more and

more things they do not need, and do not really want.

In Britain, Lord Bath and others talk nostalgically about the thirties — a time when the rich were rich, and the poor were poor, and everything was in its rightful place. "Our motto," his Lordship says, "was treat 'em mean, keep 'em keen." People did not try to overstep the line. They did not covet luxuries which the Almighty had reserved for their betters. Hence there was no need for nil norms, productivity bargaining, freezes, squeezes, courts of inquiry, and all the other nonsense which nowadays dominate the headlines. In America, students stage demonstrations against the "manipulation" of the consumer society, and particularly of leisure.

In the Soviet Union, Karl Marx's disciples have taken care not to fall into the same trap. Workers have not been spoiled by things like cars, dachas, and refrigerators. Moscow has no traffic problems because prices of the few cars made available every year are fixed at a level which the worker knows he cannot afford. A pair of shoes can cost a week's wages, so there is little left for fripperies. And you will still find several families living in one apartment, just as they used to do in Britain, because the wise men in the Kremlin recognize the need to protect the working class from the influences which are causing so much trouble here. Soviet workers are not compelled to live in degrading luxury.

Contrast this with life in unhappy America and Britain. Sprawling suburbs. Streets choked with cars. A TV set in every home. Fried chicken every day. More and more leisure. Glamorous ads enticing us to travel freely, and cheaply, around the world. If I didn't know better, I'd say it was all a communist plot, an attempt to smother us with prosperity. Some expert, no doubt, will sooner or later say it for me.

CONSUMPTION

A much misunderstood term because, in economics, it means not only things which are physically consumed — such as food — but also objects and services which are in regular use, such as furniture, and services such as transport and window-cleaning. You can "consume" a record — or this book — without actually eating it. Economists are forever trying to measure consumption, because it is so crucial to economic management. They talk about our "propensity to consume" — meaning the relationship between income and consumer spending. The "propensity" (a tendency to move in a certain direction) is subject to all kinds of influence; in some circumstances, we tend to save more than in others. The concept was evolved by Keynes and is still very much in use.

CONVENTION
See CONFERENCE.

CONVERTIBILITY

Freedom to exchange one nation's currency for another. If you travel from Britain to the United States or France you can convert your pounds into dollars or francs at the airport, or any bank. More than thirty countries have made their paper money freely convertible in this way. Many, though, apply some form of restriction on transfers of capital, and even on the total sum exchanged by travelers on each trip. And some carry their restrictions so far that, in effect, their currency is not convertible at all. They include the Iron Curtain countries and China, and poor nations who dare not risk having their citizens swap local money for so-called "hard currency." (See HARD CURRENCY.)

The term "convertibility" at one time meant convertible into gold. This is now comparatively rare. Even the United States, the richest country in the world, had to suspend convertibility when too many people tried their hand at it in the late sixties and early seventies.

CONVERTIBLE BOND
See BOND.

COOLING-OFF PERIOD
A device for getting members of a labor union back to work during an industrial dispute. Members can be ordered not to take part in any strike or employee action short of a strike during a specified period; union leaders are charged with taking all reasonable steps to insure this order is followed. The device is politically popular, but it is of doubtful industrial value, mainly because there is no guarantee whatever that it will solve a labor dispute. A cooling-off period, if fully effective, only suspends action for a time. Unless the union actually "cools off," industrial action can be restarted when the period expires.

COOPERATIVE
See CONDOMINIUM.

CORPORATE JET
Also known as "company plane." Ostensibly designed to make it possible for senior executives to keep in touch with all corners of their far-flung empire. Branch heads regard it as a nuisance, because no one likes to have the president drop in at all hours of the day. Fortunately, the corporate

jet set is always on the go: it seldom stays in one place for long. Many of the planes are converted into company offices, so that the normal routine — meetings, paperwork — can be continued without interruption. Others exist mainly to give the company the "right image": the idea is to convey the impression that it is modern, outward looking, energetic. Hugh Hefner's *Bunny* is perhaps the most prominent example. Junior executives occasionally get asked along for a free ride, and tend to regard it as a sign that they've made it to the top. It isn't. Usually it's no more than a cunning attempt by the boss to squeeze extra work out of his staff.

COST-BENEFIT ANALYSIS

A method increasingly used by governments to determine the effectiveness of public spending, in relation to costs, in meeting stated objectives. It tries to put a monetary value on services which, by their nature, have no market in which their value could otherwise be tested. A frequently cited example is highways: attempts are nowadays made to estimate the return which we, the public, get from them and compare it with alternative uses of government funds. There are, of course, considerable snags in this type of calculation and often cost-benefit analysis tends to be of little more than academic interest. Take defense: how do you calculate the benefit we derive from a nuclear submarine, or a jet fighter, or the atom bomb? They may prevent a war, but no accountant likes to put a price on something that hasn't happened, and may never happen. Still, cost-benefit analysis is an advance on the old hit-and-miss methods. Its value shouldn't be overrated, but with government spending nowadays being such a huge operation it helps to have at least *some* financial yardstick.

COST-CUTTING
Popular panic reaction to a fall in profits. Practiced with special vigor when the economy is stagnant. Frequently starts with the managing director touring the office at night, snapping off light switches and turning the heater down two degrees. Sometimes a healthy thing, because companies do get careless in their supervision of costs when business is booming. But also potentially dangerous because a sudden fury of indiscriminate cost slashing can destroy the confidence of staff and customers. Key employees may decide to seek safer jobs. Customers and suppliers may stop ordering and suppliers may refuse to give credit. Cost-cutting, moreover, usually hits sections which seem dispensable but in reality are not. Advertising, research, training programs —these tend to be among the first victims. A much more sensible policy is to keep an eye on costs all the year round, and to avoid potentially embarrassing commitments. But if you do happen to run into a madman with an ax, an effective counterploy is to send him memos listing all the savings you have made by not doing something.

The potential is truly staggering. Think of the money a company like IBM could save by not building new factories. Or the economies publishers could achieve by not producing any books. The ploy also works for governments. The secretary of the treasury could announce that he has saved us, say, ten billion dollars by not putting up taxes. And the president could tell the nation that he has saved each citizen a hundred thousand dollars by not declaring war on the Soviet Union. This could be repeated, with variations, whenever the opinion polls indicate a downturn in the administration's popularity.

COST-OF-LIVING ADJUSTMENT
See CONSUMER PRICE INDEX.

CRAWLING PEG
Basically, a way of making small and, if necessary, frequent changes, either up or down, in exchange rates. The international monetary system set up after the Second World War provided for the price of each currency to be fixed at a certain level — the pivot being the US dollar. This was supposed to be adjustable whenever it became obvious that changing circumstances had made a price unrealistic. In practice, countries proved increasingly reluctant to adjust: maintaining a fixed rate became a matter of national pride. The crawling peg theory was advocated as a means of achieving the necessary adjustment with the minimum of fuss. A major change might cause a public outcry; a crawl would go almost unnoticed. (See also FIXED PARITY and FLOATING.)

CREDIT CARD
A device to make you spend more. Surveys show that people using credit cards spend 23 per cent more than they do using cash. Money, in the old-fashioned sense of coins and notes, is out of date. It certainly is no longer a status symbol: Americans who insist on settling bills in cash are increasingly regarded with suspicion. They look like have-nots who cannot be trusted with charge accounts and credit cards. One does not need a wallet full of dollar bills these days to travel around the United States. Indeed, it is advisable — because it is safer — to leave your wallet at home. Hotels, department stores, gas stations, car rental agencies,

restaurants, airlines, and many others have all got away from paper money. Even ambulance services and mortuaries take credit cards, and there's a sign outside a San Francisco church which proclaims that your card is good for the collection plate. If it were not for the tiresome necessity of tipping doormen and cab drivers, America would be closer still to fulfillment of the ultimate dream: a cashless society. In Britain we have been somewhat slower to change our ways, but no one would dispute that things are not what they were. The banks, which used to be so stuffy, have joined the credit card boom with surprising enthusiasm. There are bankers who believe that, by the end of the century, we may be able to dispense with coins and bank notes altogether. This may strike you as far-fetched, but, if you look at the change in attitudes — and customs — over the past thirty years, it seems by no means impossible that cash will eventually become obsolete. It is already feasible, if you are so minded, to live without ever touching a single dollar bill. The check has long ceased to be a novelty, even among the working class, and the stigma once attached to borrowing is gone for good. Anyone who suggests, today, that installment buying is immoral would be dismissed as a crank. The pay envelope still exists, but millions now have their earnings paid directly into a bank and write checks against the money. Expense account living merely requires a signature. Travelers' checks are as widely used as season tickets and credit cards. In short, one can get by on bookkeeping transactions. There is no doubt that we shall travel further along this road. The process will be hastened by inflation, as it has been already. As money buys less and less, the conventional coinage and currency will seem more and more inappropriate. For banks and traders, handling currency is expensive, time-consuming, and unhygienic. The printing of bills and the manufacture of coins involve considerable cost. So does the elaborate business of moving the currency around the country, with the constant necessity of counting it, packing it, and protecting it. Theoretically, there is no need for any of this. All that matters is that people should be ready and willing to accept whatever form of payment is in fashion. It's not the money as such that counts, but what it will buy.

CREDIT UNION
A "cooperative society" whose function is to encourage members to save systematically and to make personal loans to them in times of need. Credit unions are private organizations, owned and operated by the members. They are usually organized among employees in industry or by occupational groups such as schoolteachers and others with a common bond. Members in most instances are shareholders, not depositors or creditors. They save by buying shares in the association. Loans are made out of the accumulated savings fund: US law allows unsecured loans of up to $750 and adequately secured loans in larger amounts, depending on the size of the credit union. Shareholders often get free life insurance; against this, their shares are not insured as are deposits in other banking institutions.

CRITICAL PATH ANALYSIS
An impressive way of saying that you are going to look at something in detail. The idea is to (a) break it down into component parts and (b) examine each part both in isolation and in its relationship to the other parts. Hopefully, this will show how a given project can be finished in the best possible way in the quickest possible time. For example, if you are building a factory a critical path analysis will reveal

that you should concrete the floor before the machinery is delivered, but after you've laid the drains! Anyone who has dealt with the building industry will know that this principle is not as widely accepted as it should be.

CYCLICAL STOCKS
Stocks of companies which go with "feast or famine" swings in their respective industries. They include the steel, automobiles, housing, machine tool, and hotel industries. Some analysts believe the list should also include companies which depend heavily on Washington's willingness and ability to advance money: aerospace is given as the most obvious example.

Individual stocks may move against the general trend, at least for a while, but as a rule the label "cyclical" is well deserved.

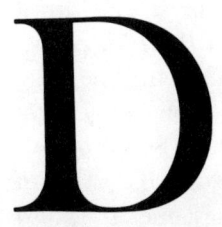

D

DATA
Fancy substitute — it comes from the Latin *datum* — for the more familiar word "facts." I don't know who first decided that it sounded more imposing, but it has certainly caught on in a most remarkable way. Advertising and marketing

men are particularly fond of it. You should certainly know the difference between hard data and soft data: the one means numerical measurements and the other "insights which are not expressible in numerical terms," such as the "personality" of a newspaper.

DEBENTURES
Stocks issued by a company in return for long-term loans. They are a debt on the company and, as with a mortgage, are normally secured on part or all of the fixed assets such as property, plant, and machinery. Debentures are entitled to a fixed rate of interest, which has to be paid whether the company makes enough profits or not. If the company doesn't have the funds, debenture holders can foreclose, put it into receivership, or take other action to protect their interests. In short, they are the safest form of stock on the market. Some may be redeemed (repaid) at a specific date or over a stated number of years, and others may be irredeemable, meaning that the capital is not repaid unless and until the company goes out of business. Debentures are popular with investors who want to combine safety with a reasonable rate of income. But they don't share in profits and, therefore, are no safeguard against inflation. The market price, moreover, depends to some extent on the general level of interest prevailing at any given time. So even with debentures there is no absolute guarantee that the value of your investment will always stay exactly the same. (See also BOND.)

DEBTOR
A person who owes money to another. The stigma once attached to debt has long disappeared; nowadays everyone runs up debts at one time or another. Personally I would

much rather be a debtor than a creditor, especially at times of rapid inflation. Say you borrow $10,000 and undertake to pay it back in five years' time. If you invest it wisely, the chances are that the value of your holding, at the end of that period, will show an increase which will not only make up for the interest you have paid on the loan, but will also give you a useful capital gain. Your repayment will be exactly $10,000, plus interest, but in terms of purchasing power that sum will be worth a lot less than it was five years earlier. In short, you are repaying in devalued currency. During that five years, moreover, the creditor has a vested interest in your financial health. A bank manager who has helped to set you up in business will want to protect his loan: the chances are that, if you run into temporary financial difficulty, he will give you further assistance rather than risk losing the money altogether. A creditor (i.e., a person to whom money is owed) is in a strong legal position, and in theory can recover his loan at any given time. In practice, though, he tends to be much more at the mercy of events than is generally acknowledged. (See also BAD DEBTS.)

DE-ESCALATE

Reduce. A favorite with labor union leaders and others. A top official, not long ago, said he would "do his best to stop the escalation of official action."

He wouldn't dream of talking like that to his wife or friends, but somehow it seems to be assumed that plain English won't do on these occasions. A *Financial Times* reader pointed out, cheekily, that the word "de-escalate" means to "incorporate mission constraints on a reducing basis, independent of functional principles." Well, yes, certainly. But how about a meaningful de-escalation of jargon, or, putting it another way, a spot of dejargonization?

DEFICIT SPENDING
See PUMP PRIMING.

DENIAL
Firm insistence that a rumor is incorrect. Seldom accepted at its face value. It's taken for granted that every businessman, or economist, or politician tells lies from time to time. Not only taken for granted, but excused on the grounds that, if everyone went around telling the truth on each and every occasion, society as we know it would be in mortal danger. Journalists have long worked on the premise that when a man says one thing, he usually means exactly the opposite.

In the United States politicians aspiring to the White House invariably announce that they are not candidates, which means that they most certainly are. In the business world, you can usually tell that a deal is on the point of being clinched by the vigor of the denials that anything is going on at all. There are, alas, a few people who do not, as yet, appear to know about the new convention. They continue to issue denials in the old-fashioned expectation that everyone will accept them as the last word. The denials confuse those who have come to regard them as the most reliable form of confirmation, and it may be helpful to provide a brief guideline:

(1) If you want people to think that you didn't do it, issue a public statement saying that you did. Then no one will believe you.

(2) If you want to take credit for something that has gone well, deny that you have had anything to do with it. Then journalists will automatically assume that you are merely being modest.

(3) If you don't want people to know about a deal that's still in the pipeline, do not on any account issue a denial. Say, "Sure, and I'm taking over General Motors and IBM as well." Wall Street will take that as a clear sign that you're not involved in negotiations of any kind.

(4) If you want to leak some piece of good news, tell it to a friend in "strict confidence," and sit by your telephone waiting for the inevitable call from the journalist. Pretend to be surprised and disconcerted, and issue a vague denial. He will then realize that he's got a scoop, and the news will be splashed on page one. If you merely make a public announcement, it will be tucked away at the bottom of page 14.

There are various well-established phrases to use on all these occasions, and you ought to know at least a few of them.

"This is absolutely untrue" means "Yes, it's true, but you don't expect me to say so, do you?" A variation of this is "I don't know what you are talking about." It means he hopes you, the questioner, don't know what you're talking about. "This is absurd" means "He is on to something there." And "Yes, we are negotiating with IBM" means "No, we're not, but we would like to."

DEPRECIATION
See WASTING ASSETS.

DEPRESSION
A word which will always be associated, in most people's minds, with the Great Crash of 1929. Actually, it means "large fall in output and employment." The Great Crash

was a financial breakdown which led to a breakdown in the economy. One fourth of the labor force was unemployed and industrial production cut in half, a situation that dragged on year after year. The economic distress extended to Europe, Asia, Africa, Australia, and South America. Economists were bewildered: they had no explanations and no remedies. Recovery was slow and owed a good deal to the "new economics" pioneered by John Maynard Keynes (see KEYNES). Today the term is often used rather indiscriminately. People talk of "depression" and "slump" when they really mean "recession" or "slowdown."

DEVALUATION

Reducing the value of a country's currency in terms of foreign currencies.

In 1967, Britain devalued by 14.3 per cent — meaning that, henceforth, the pound would buy that much less in terms of dollars. Devaluation makes it cheaper for foreigners to buy our products, and eventually leads to bigger exports. But it also means that we have to pay more for everything we buy abroad, including food. A country which frequently devalues, moreover, finds that foreign traders lose confidence in its paper money. They exchange it for something else — gold, or raw materials — as quickly as they can. No one wants to be stuck with paper which can lose its value overnight.

Devaluation also has a more indirect effect on confidence at home: the higher cost of imports after 1967 and the publicity given to the "downfall" of the pound are widely believed to have triggered off the severe bout of inflation which followed. This is why the Bank of England and others strongly disapprove of devaluation. Many economists do not agree. They argue that, once it is clear that a country's currency is no longer worth the price asked for it, it's best to devalue at once rather than go through the long and tiresome business of defending the existing exchange rate. They say that Mr. Wilson — and later General de Gaulle — made the mistake of turning a fixed exchange rate into a national prestige symbol. "The pound," Mr. Wilson announced in 1964, "is in danger." By implication, the country was in danger too. We were fighting for survival. This, economists maintain, is arrant nonsense. A nation's survival does not depend on its ability to maintain a certain rate against the dollar, and to invoke Dunkirk in such situation is bogus patriotism.

DIMINISHING RETURNS (LAW OF)
A phrase you simply must know if you want to show that you understand economics. The law is relatively simple: at a certain point it does not pay to add to the effort to improve, say, a piece of land. Additional outlay does not correspondingly increase the return. Carried far enough, it will reduce it. The law also applies to other activities, notably the raising of taxes. A government cannot tax, say, tobacco or drinks ad infinitum. Sooner or later it reaches the point where another increase produces such a sharp fall in sales that, on balance, the extra tax produces very little extra revenue or actually leads to a drop in the overall income.

DISCOUNT
Basically a reduction in a previously determined price. In the stock market, it may refer to the difference between the price at which a stock was issued and the price at which it now stands, if the latter is the lower. In business, it may be

the amount deducted from the face value of a bill of exchange (see page 22) or another promise-to-pay note for cashing it in advance of the date when it's due for repayment. Financial institutions will often take bills over from their owners, pay the owners cash which they may need rather badly, and take a chance with the bill in return for a cut known as the "discount rate."

For the rest of us, discount tends to be much more simple. It's the amount that a retail store, or some other business, is prepared to knock off the advertised price in order to get our trade. Discount stores generally work on the basis of a smaller profit on a greater volume of sales: the reasoning is that, at the end of the day, they will turn out to have done at least as well as their competitors. But of course the system is open to abuse; sometimes stores are simply selling inferior goods.

In some countries of the world "discount" is very much part of everyday life. I have a small house in Sicily and do a lot of shopping there. Chain stores apart, the first question you are expected to ask is "How much discount?" Everyone knows that, if the goods you see in the window are priced at all, it will be at a deliberately exaggerated figure. Having asked the customary question you must then throw up your hands in horror when you get the shopkeeper's answer. "Mamma mia," you say, deeply shocked, and prepare to walk out. He will then call you back (or, if not, you try returning an hour or so later) and give you a more realistic price. If you're really determined you usually spend another half an hour haggling. It's all very silly, really, and I find it a bore, but getting the right sort of discount tends to be a matter of honor — and in Sicily, honor is all.

There are many ways of securing a discount in the United States, and one of my favorites is to wave a credit card in front of the store owner or manager — and then offer not to use it. The bank or credit card company that has given that card to you insists on a kickback of up to 7 per cent and the card's sole justification, as far as the store is concerned, is that it attracts business. The shopkeeper loses nothing if he gives you a similar discount on a cash purchase, and is actually better off if you settle for less. Don't try it with airlines, railroads, or big restaurants; nor with small shopkeepers who need your business and have the authority to make their own prices.

DISCOUNTED CASH FLOW
See CASH FLOW.

DISCOUNTING NEWS
Newcomers to investment are sometimes surprised to find that the stock market's reaction to good news is the opposite of what they had expected: a higher dividend may actually be followed by a decline in price. This is because the market has already "discounted" the news, meaning that it has correctly anticipated what the company concerned will do. Any well-known growth stock is closely followed by a lot of people, and professionals usually have a fairly good idea what to expect. It doesn't always happen, of course, and the discounting process also works in the case of bad news. A dividend cut may have been allowed for several weeks in advance (nervous people will have sold their stock) and the actual announcement will be greeted with relief that the setback has not proved any bigger. With the worst known, new buyers may well be attracted by the possibility that, next year, the former rate will be restored. Company boards often regard it as a matter of pride to make good a dividend cut at the earliest opportunity.

Discounting, of course, also happens in the market as a whole. The stock exchange usually runs ahead of the economy, or individual industries, and a pickup in profits may well be allowed for months ahead of the published confirmation.

DISINVESTMENT
Getting rid of losers. A lot of corporations rush into acquisitions and mergers which, within a year or so, turn out to be ill advised. They swallow up capital, don't contribute enough to group profits, and tie up management which could be more usefully employed elsewhere. Disinvestment takes courage, because it generally means having to admit that you've made a mistake. Some companies funk it and eventually find themselves dragged down by the ailing member. Others rightly consider it part of normal business strategy.

DIVERSIFICATION
Spreading your risk by making several products, investing in different stocks, or moving into new fields through the acquisition of other companies. The stock market is understandably cautious about "one-product firms" because conditions can so easily turn against them. The John Bloom crash in Britain, some years ago, is a frequently quoted example. Bloom started with a good idea. It was not particularly original or complicated. But he pushed forward with supreme self-confidence and energetic enthusiasm, and the idea caught on brilliantly. Britain's washing-machine giants were selling their products through the shops, handing retailers a large profit margin. Bloom eliminated the re-

tailer, and went all out for big sales. He used every gimmick in the book, and a few new ones, to build up the kind of volume he wanted. But to become a really big tycoon, running a business that will last, you need more than a single idea. You can spot a gap in big industry's armor and exploit it vigorously, but as soon as you've proved yourself you must look around for fresh fields to conquer. Bloom realized the dangers of sticking exclusively to the washing-machine business once the slumbering giants had been awakened. He desperately tried to repeat his success in other fields. But he was impatient, and he reveled in publicity. When the crash came he was in Bulgaria, of all places, trying to fix up a contract for package tours. It never got off the ground.

Many well-known highly respectable companies have also found that successful diversification is easier said than done. Distillers, world-famous for its brands of whiskey and gin, launched out into the industrial field many years ago and built up a separate chemicals division. Not long ago, however, the directors gladly sold the major part of the group's chemical interests to British Petroleum — and announced that they planned to plow the money back into their traditional liquor business. Guinness has built up extensive interests in the confectionery business through the acquisition of various companies, but is still very much on the "one product" hook. British American Tobacco acquired the Yardley cosmetics firm in 1967, and also the Toni-bell ice-cream business. Imperial Tobacco, worried by the declining scope for its principal product, went into potato chips, teaching machines, and electronic equipment. All would, I am sure, readily admit that diversification is full of pitfalls.

DIVIDEND
The income stockholders get on their investments. In theory, dividends on common stock reflect the company's prosperity, going up in a good year and down in a bad one. But it doesn't always work that way. A company may maintain its dividend rate during a temporary setback, because it values its stock market reputation. Similarly, it may keep its dividend unchanged during a temporary upswing. There's no firm rule: companies are not *obliged* to pay dividends on common stock, and some pay nothing at all. Dividend policy clearly influences the market price of a stock, but don't automatically assume that a company which keeps all its money in the till is unpopular with stockholders. Some investors actually prefer companies which never pay a dividend. These are, as a rule, fast-growing concerns which plow back all their earnings into new factories or new products. The growth is reflected in the market price of the stock — a fact which pleases those who are more interested in capital gain than highly taxed income. I once went to the annual meeting of a company whose boss announced, sternly, that the board would "never pay a dividend while *I'm* alive." He wasn't lynched; on the contrary, those present cheered. (See also GROWTH STOCKS.)

DOLLAR IMPERIALISM
Another way of saying, "We take your cash, but we don't like it." The phrase is a firm favorite with left-wing students and others who claim that America has tried to build an empire with money. Hitting at US investment has long been fashionable all over the world; the late General de Gaulle was simply one of the more prominent attackers. But dollar imperialism is also reckoned to work through for-

eign aid. America, it's said, uses aid to maintain a position of influence and control around the world. Washington takes little trouble to deny it: economic assistance is felt to be a useful method of sustaining countries which might otherwise pass into the communist bloc. In short, to the White House dollar imperialism is a virtue; to its critics, it's a vice. There are times when Congress, reflecting the mood of a large segment of the American public, finds it all too much and votes to reduce foreign aid — or even to eliminate it altogether. This happened in 1971, and is primarily an expression of resentment against "ungrateful allies." Aid, a senator declared, "has for too long been regarded as a bottomless pit for free-loading nations who victimize Uncle Sucker."

Americans have always had a great need for affection and approval. They expect gratitude and love and they get criticism and hostility. It is a reaction with which older nations, like Britain, are more than familiar. No one ever really loves a lender. His generosity is welcomed at first, but then the recipient gives way to suspicion and resentment. People don't like to be dependent on someone else. And they certainly don't want constant reminders that they have had to accept charity. Some of the strongest attacks on dollar imperialism have come from countries who would be far worse off without it. It's a phenomenon, of course, which is familiar to individuals as well as governments: the quickest way to lose a friend is to help him get started in business, or to tide him over a bad patch.

DOLLAR PREMIUM
Anyone buying dollar stocks from London has to use special "investment dollars." As there is a limited supply, the investor has to pay a premium for them. This can amount to

30 per cent or more, and therefore represents a considerable handicap to investing on Wall Street.

DOW-JONES
Shorthand for the Dow-Jones index, Wall Street's best-known barometer. It is named after Charles H. Dow and Edward D. Jones, cofounders of the *Wall Street Journal*, who started to compile daily averages of stock prices in 1897. Dow-Jones now consists of four averages: one for 30 industrials, one for 20 rails, one for 15 utilities, and a 65-stock composite of these three groups. The averages are calculated and announced every half-hour during the New York Exchange trading day.

The Dow theory is based on the view that an index of stocks and shares reflects all that is generally known about the outlook for business in general, and expresses all the hopes and fears about the prospects for the individual companies whose stocks make up the index. Movements of Dow's indices were analyzed and it was found that certain patterns tended to repeat themselves, so that it was possible to predict future index movements with some degree of success. Some modern analysts are skeptical about the value of this approach, and it is certainly possible to make out a case against some of the claims made by Dow enthusiasts. But the indices themselves have acquired such a wide following, and have such an important psychological impact, that they are unquestionably a major factor on Wall Street.

DUMPING
A term used in international trade to describe the unloading of a particular product in another country at a low price. A company in, say, Britain may find its own market

so saturated that it prefers to "dump" a sizable part of its output in the United States or in Europe at a low profit rather than at none at all. Or it may have such a monopoly position at home that it can get away with restricting home sales, charging a high price, and dumping the rest abroad at a price which the local producer simply cannot afford to match.

There are all kinds of international agreements to prevent this sort of thing, and in practice deliberate large-scale dumping is by no means easy. It usually needs the cooperation — or, at least, compliance — of one's own government, and everyone involved knows there is always a risk of retaliation. Communist countries are clearly well placed to go in for dumping, but since most of their trade with the West is regulated by quotas they tend not to get away with it. With others, the dividing line between dumping and stiff competition may be rather thin — and one often hears cries of "unfair, unfair" when all that's really happening is that a foreign competitor is more efficient than the local firm.

E

ECONOMIC CRISIS

Every Englishman's favorite phrase. No one does a crisis as well as we do. The Americans may be better at riots, and the Danes superior at pornography, but when it comes to an economic crisis Britain is well out in front.

And so, of course, we should be. Who, after all, has had more experience? We have had an economic crisis for as long as anyone can remember; it is a British institution. The language of crisis is ours: "Export or die," the "trade gap," and the "Dunkirk spirit" are all British inventions. And no one has spent as much time pulling up socks, tightening belts, rolling up sleeves, and putting backs to the wall. Without the British economic crisis, no one would ever have heard of the Gnomes of Zürich, central bankers, and the International Monetary Fund. It would never have occurred to anyone that nations must export or die. Trade gaps and balance of payments would have remained undiscovered. No wonder foreign TV crews and newspapermen flock here to observe what has become known, throughout the world, as the "English sickness." Everyone wants to know how we do it, and how we manage to keep it up. From a TV producer's point of view, of course, an economic crisis tends to produce certain technical difficulties. It's easy enough to assemble a few experts in the studio and let them ramble on for an hour or so. But if you send a crew out on location, you have to find something they can point their cameras at. And that leaves out things like a balance-of-payments deficit. In Britain, happily, this tends to be less of a problem than in other countries. There is a routine schedule, used countless times, which can be completed in three days, and which looks something like this:

> **First day:** Morning at Buckingham Palace, to film the Changing of the Guard. This establishes that Britain is still obsessed by tradition, and totally out of touch with the twentieth century. Nice shots of horses, soldiers, et cetera. Afternoon in factory on outskirts of London, to film British workers drinking tea. This shows that the British are lazy, and explains why Britain has fallen behind in the rat race.

Second day: Morning in Hyde Park, filming labor union demonstration. This shows that when they are not drinking tea, English workers are marching up and down, shouting slogans and singing the "Red Flag." Excellent shots of Pakistanis and West Indians marching by their side; this shows that immigrants can't help catching the English disease. Afternoon in hired studio, filming interview with politician or economist who will confirm that the British economic crisis is still going strong — that, indeed, Britain is down and out, finished. This establishes the crew's impartiality.

Third day: Morning in Carnaby Street to film British decadence. Wonderful shots of girls in hot pants. This establishes that the British do not care about their economic problems — that they are only interested in having fun. Afternoon in Soho taking shots of lines outside strip clubs for extra emphasis.

The schedule, as you can see, allows a crew to collect enough material for an hour's in-depth study of a derelict empire. It is not necessary, as a rule, to send your commentator along as well, because he can get most of his opinions from the British press. There will, inevitably, be people who seek to spoil everything by claiming that, for a relatively small country, we don't do at all badly. There may even be some who argue that Britain is a more pleasant country to live in than economically successful societies like the United States and Japan. The younger generation, particularly, seems to be prone to this kind of dangerous thinking. Fortunately, our own press can be relied upon to attack such foolish notions. Britain without a crisis is nothing at all: sackcloth and ashes are our national dress, and misery — pretended or otherwise — our most valued tradition.

ECONOMIC GROWTH

Economic development, or more accurately the outward signs of development — expansion in employment, capital, the volume of trade and consumption. Its main objective is, of course, to raise the general standard of living. Comparatively few people know how it is measured, and among those who do there are doubts about the value of some of the calculations. But it is generally accepted as the most important single yardstick. (See also GROSS NATIONAL PRODUCT, simply another way of saying the same thing.) A growth rate of 2 to 3 per cent, such as Britain has had in recent years, is considered poor. The United States has a better track record, but the real pacesetter has been Japan. Between 1955 and 1965, its growth rate averaged 9.7 per cent, which by common consent qualifies for a tag "miracle." Key factors making for rapid growth include expansionist government politics, good business management, improved labor training, and a high level of investment in new plant and machinery.

ECONOMIC MAN
A mythical creature, used as a convenient abstraction in discussing economic affairs. Economists, as a rule, ground their theories chiefly on how rational people might behave in a certain situation on the basis of certain assumptions. The main assumption is that Economic Man has an overwhelming urge to maximize his wealth with the minimum of sacrifice. This is enshrined in hundreds of textbooks: if X happens, Y is supposed to follow.

The trouble is that comparatively few people read the textbooks. Most people are guided by instinct rather than knowledge. And instinct frequently makes them go in for behavior which, to the academic, seems bewilderingly irrational. This might not matter so much if conditions were still the same as twenty or thirty years ago. The textbooks suggest plenty of ways in which people can be brought to heel. But conditions are not the same. Economists all over the world admit that they have not yet learned to cope with the combined force of affluence, bloodymindedness, and labor union power. Economic Man frequently acts in a way which appears to run counter to his best interests: he prefers leisure to making more money, brings his employers (and himself) to ruin by indulging in pointless strikes, and panics when common sense requires that he should be calm. Younger Economic Man also tends to react differently from older Economic Man. He is, for example, less easily shaken by the threat of unemployment. It's not just that greatly improved unemployment benefits have taken away some of the sting. A more potent influence is, quite simply, that workers who have not experienced conditions like those of the thirties are less easily frightened than those who have.

ECONOMIES OF SCALE

The benefits of size. A supermarket chain which can buy in bulk gets economies of scale which are denied to the small shopkeeper. A manufacturer operating in, say, the motor industry can reduce the cost of each new car through long runs of output or standardized parts. This has been the reasoning behind the merger boom of recent years: larger units, it has been argued, are more able to take on foreign competition than small ones. There is, clearly, a great deal to be said for this kind of thinking. The economies of scale are not a pipe dream. But experience suggests that they often take a good deal longer to achieve than direction would have investors believe at the time of the merger. And size can produce all kinds of problems. Size alone is certainly no guarantee of greater efficiency.

The advantages of scale, if they are not to be outweighed by the disadvantages, are not automatic, but have to be worked for in a climate of sustained economic expansion. They can only be gained if plants are working at, or near, full capacity. There's also the question of market power; in many cases, it is against the interest of consumers — which means you and me — to have any one firm gain too much of a hold on any particular trade or industry.

EFFICIENCY

Today's watchword — it's what the other fellow doesn't have enough of. Politicians find it a useful peg for noncommittal speeches, and company chairmen like to include it in their annual statements on the principle that if you talk about it loud enough no one will suspect *you* of shortcomings. No businessman, of course, admits to being inefficient — and why should he? As long as you are making money, it's all a matter of opinion. It's easy to hit up new profit peaks each year by employing more and more capital (plenty of firms get a reputation for efficiency that way) and it isn't hard to convince yourself that, if your earnings are not all they should be, it is purely because you have a decent sense of priority. Staff and customers come before profit: you are a modern manager.

Prosperous trading conditions do not make for maximum efficiency. When business is booming, all sorts of things go unnoticed. Parkinson's law tends to work overtime: every petty section head can quietly add one or two people to the staff. New ventures are looked at less critically and old machinery is kept working flat out. No one wants to risk disruption when order books stretch way ahead. A different attitude tends to develop when business slackens and profit margins come under pressure; suddenly, boards start to ask themselves questions. There's nothing like a good, old-fashioned setback to make company directors doubt their own genius.

ENTREPRENEUR

One who undertakes an enterprise; an individual who owns the business and takes the risk. You will come across the word in economics textbooks, but just about the only people who use it nowadays are economists and financial writers. Even in France, an entrepreneur is more commonly referred to as *le businessman*. The entrepreneurial function is held to be a central concept in economics, and many theories are built on it. Some still hold water, but others have been outdated by drastic changes in industrial structure — the managers who now run the biggest companies are not entrepreneurs in the original sense.

EQUITY

Another name for "common stocks." They are the risk capital, taking the benefits if things go well, and shouldering all or the bulk of the loss if they go badly. Most companies have loan capital, preferred shares, or some other stock which has prior claim on both earnings and assets. Interest and dividends on these have to be paid out of the year's profits before anything is made available for distribution to equity holders. If the company should go bust, equity holders are last in line. Because of this, common stocks are generally more subject to price fluctuations than debentures or preferred shares. Their main attraction is that, unlike the others, they share in the company's prosperity. They also have a vote, which means they are the bosses. Well, that's the theory anyway. In practice, things tend to be a bit more complicated.

Few companies pay out all their surplus in the form of dividends. A board of directors may, for example, decide that it needs a big part of the surplus to finance expansion or modernization. The dividend will, in that case, be kept at the same level even though the company may have had an excellent year. The equity holder ultimately benefits, because the company is — or should be — enhancing its earnings power and adding to the assets backing for the shares. But it could mean a temporary setback in the share price.

As an owner, the equity holder is free to complain. But it is by no means easy to take on the board of one of today's big corporations — unless, perhaps, you have 15 or 20 per cent of the equity. Just about the only time when your vote really counts is during a take-over battle, when equity holders tend to be wooed by both sides with considerable ardor. (See also ANNUAL GENERAL MEETING.)

ERGONOMICS

The scientific study of ordinary people in work situations. The word has become fashionable with the advent of "behavioral science." Today's conditions, of course, are a marked improvement on the time when twelve-year-old children were sent down a mine, regardless of human consequences. Ergonomics, and/or behavioral science, tries to apply modern methods to the design of processes and machines, to the layout of work places, to methods of work, and to "job satisfaction," in order to get greater efficiency of both men and machines. In short, it acknowledges the importance of people in the moneymaking process. The trouble is that workers often behave in an illogical, contradictory way. Bloodymindedness, for example, constantly gets in the way of theories. One result is that, as with economics, scientists often give up the struggle and stick to theorizing or writing papers for examiners and other practitioners in the field. (See also ECONOMIC MAN and IN-PLANT FEEDING SITUATION.)

ESCALATOR CLAUSE

Any clause in a contract which allows the supplier to revise his terms upward because of changed circumstances. Say you have ordered an expensive piece of machinery, for delivery in a year's time. The manufacturer has agreed to a certain price, and you both have a contract. If he is smart — and can get away with it — he will also have worked in an escalator clause making it possible to pass on, say, an increase in costs of raw materials and labor during that time.

Labor-management contracts sometimes have an escalator clause which calls for an increase in wages as the cost-of-living index rises. Landlords, too, frequently build such clauses into leases.

ESCHEAT

An old legal term for the right to seize property which has no apparent owner. It often happens with unclaimed bank deposits; in New York, for example, the state may grab the money in a forgotten or overlooked bank account after ten years. The bank will generally try to reach a depositor by writing to his last known address, or by advertising in a newspaper, but if that fails the bank is legally obliged to hand the funds over.

In theory, it is possible for, say, a bank robber to open an account in another state and deposit a large amount of cash without telling a soul. He is arrested a few months later and sentenced to fifteen years in prison. He can't tell the bank his new address because, if he does, the police would probably discover his secret cache. So he sits in his cell, biting his fingernails, knowing that after ten years the money will go to the state. I don't know whether anything like this has happened — but it makes a good plot for a novel, don't you think?

EURO-BOND MARKET

Set up in 1963, it has established itself as the most versatile (and volatile) capital market in Europe. Like the Euro-dollar, it owes its existence largely to US government restrictions designed to help the US balance of payments. US firms tried to raise money in Europe instead, and the Euro-bond made its appearance. The market is chiefly meant for businessmen who want to borrow for periods of ten years or more, and is used by many other people besides the Americans. Its growth was helped by the narrowness of continental money markets, and today it overshadows all national centers — accommodating a wider range of borrowers than any other. Investors, too, find advantages in buying Euro-bonds and there is now a Euro-dollar equity — suitable for American companies wishing to raise funds overseas.

At first, Euro-bonds were nearly always issued in Euro-dollars. This meant that any investor in any European country who had Euro-dollars could buy the issue. More recently, Euro-bonds have also been issued in other European currencies which have established their strength and general acceptability — notably the German mark.

EURO-DOLLARS

A controversial "currency" which did not really make an impact until the mid-fifties, but then had a spectacular career. They are, basically, dollars accumulated in Europe from large American overseas net lending and spending. The dollars found their way into Europe's commercial banks, and eventually a market was established in them. The Euro-dollar market was given a big boost in 1968, when President Johnson put controls on further dollar outflows for investment in Europe. American firms tried to find dollars anywhere they could, especially in Europe. But Americans were by no means the only people interested in Euro-dollars; because they had the advantage of being instantly accepted in every country, and of not being subject to any central control, Euro-dollars appealed to businessmen in many other nations. Critics say the Euro-dollar has added to inflation, and has led to increased speculation. They look forward to the day when Europe introduces its own currency; if and when that happens, the role of the Euro-dollar will be severely diminished, if not ended altogether. Meanwhile, other Euro-currencies, notably the German mark, are increasingly challenging the Euro-dollar's position as the most generally accepted paper money. (See also EURO-BONDS and EUROPEAN MONETARY UNION.)

EUROPEAN (THE)

A term which used to mean "colonial administrator" but now denotes someone who believes in the Common Market. Churchill had a vision, back in 1948, of the true European. "I hope," he said, "to see a Europe where men and women of every country will think as much of being European as of belonging to their native land, and wherever they go in this wide domain will truly feel 'here I am at home.'" The only people who are like that, in fact, are the Eurocrats in Brussels, the young men and women who prefer travel to a dull job at home, and the Americans who work in a European city. For a decade or so after the last world war, the Germans and, to a lesser extent the Italians, tried to hide their shame by professing to be Europeans. With the war almost forgotten, they do so no longer. Nationalism has come into its own again.

The young, on the whole, feel more at home in Europe than anyone else. They did not experience the last two wars, and care remarkably little about them. They do not see Germans or Italians as enemies, and are much more inclined to regard the beaches of Italy or France as common property. Like Henry Ford, they tend to feel that history is bunk. Napoleon's battles have the same ludicrous ring about them as those old newsreel films of the Nuremberg rallies and other displays of patriotic fervor which inspired earlier generations. Europe looks a good deal smaller to the twenty-year-old of today than it did to his father and grandfather. It will look smaller still to *his* sons — though it will be a very long time before anyone introduces himself at a party with the words: "Hallo, I'm a European." To the Chinese,of course, all distinctions are academic: to them, all Europeans look the same.

EUROPEAN ECONOMIC COMMUNITY (EEC)
See COMMON MARKET.

EUROPEAN MONETARY UNION
A concept cherished by those who believe that there's more to creating a United Europe than making pious speeches. The aim is an integrated money and capital market within the EEC, and a common currency. In other words, businessmen in EEC countries should be able to borrow wherever they like, without interference, and EEC countries should all be able to use the same kind of money. The Six have actually agreed on a three-stage plan toward full monetary union by 1980, but this is generally thought to be far too optimistic. The trouble is, as usual, that politicians find things much more difficult than the theorists. There has never been any shortage of plans; the only problem has been a shortage of desire to make them work.

The Common Market is the biggest trading bloc in the world, and it clearly makes sense to establish a European money market and a European currency. There are frequent meetings of all the ministers concerned; there is even a European Parliament where, in theory, differences can be sorted out in a democratic manner. But individual countries, notably France, have not yet made up their minds what kind of Europe they really want. They want to enjoy the advantages which the EEC offers, but dislike the idea of handing over national sovereignty to a European body. Progress, therefore, has been slow. There have been useful steps, such as the creation of a European Currency Unit — defined in terms of gold to be the same weight as the dollar, and used in money-raising operations by bodies such as the European Coal and Steel Community. But as a rule, meetings to discuss really important moves have ended either in disarray, or in compromise solutions forced upon the EEC by some US initiative. Some experts think that Britain's entry into the Common Market will insure faster progress; others argue that it will merely widen the scope for disagreement.

EXCHANGE CONTROL
An official attempt to regulate the amount of money going in and out of a country. The motive is simple enough — governments are not content to leave the rate which a currency may command abroad at the mercy of free market forces. They may genuinely want to keep exchange rates stable, or they may think it advisable to operate with an undervalued currency in order to make exports competitive. Britain has long had an elaborate system of exchange control, and a full list of all the regulations would fill a separate book. Treasury and Bank of England officials responsible

for administering the system have admitted to me that even they don't know all of its rules. You can't have a bank account abroad without government permission, or use your own money to buy property anywhere outside the Sterling Area, unless the Bank of England gives official approval. You can't hold certain foreign securities, or buy gold, without special authority. I am giving you just a few of the more obvious examples; the whole exchange control field is a bureaucratic paradise.

Under the Common Market rules, we are supposed to get some major changes. One of the aims of the Common Market, after all, is to remove artificial barriers within Europe. Experience suggests, however, that officials are reluctant to relinquish entrenched positions and that politicians tend to give in to them. The public, on the whole, does not seem to care enough to apply real pressure. The only measure of exchange control which has caught the imagination, over the past decade, was the 1964–1970 Labour Government's introduction of a £50 travel allowance. Jim Callaghan, the Chancellor responsible, has since told me that I put the idea into his head in a long article I wrote for the *Manchester Guardian*. It's enough to make one want to give up writing.

EXECUTIVE

A man who talks to visitors while the employees get their work done. "Executive" was once a high status word, designating the top people in a corporation — from departmental heads upward. Today it is applied much more generously. Anyone whose office duties require him to supervise the work of at least one other person has nowadays some claim to being called an executive. A higher executive can usually boast of a generous expense account, a company car, and a key to the executive lavatory. But the boundaries are getting blurred: expense accounts are not so difficult to come by, and even the newest office recruit, sharing a secretary with a colleague, can usually get away with calling himself an executive. He may have to settle at first for "junior executive," but this stage usually doesn't last very long. Top management, anxious to keep ahead, usually likes to be known as "senior executives." But the most coveted title is chief executive: it's the one label which still means what it says.

Car manufacturers, airlines, railways, magazines, and many others have done their best to exploit the executive boom. You don't have to be an executive to own an executive car, or to take an executive trip. Or, for that matter, to read this — which is, of course, an executive book.

EXECUTOR

No one has yet devised an effective way of taking it with you, but an executor will insure that what you leave behind doesn't fall into the hands of the wrong people. The first step is to make a will; if that sounds morbid and defeatist, remember that we've all got to go eventually and dying intestate (that is, without making a will) may cause your relatives a lot of quite unnecessary trouble and expense. A will allows you to select your own executor, and many people automatically pick husband, wife, or grown-up son or daughter. Another possibility is a family friend with experience in business, finance, or the law: a frequent choice is that of the solicitor who has drawn up the will. The larger banks all have executor and trustee departments which, like solicitors, will take on the job for a fee. If you have reason to think that your relatives might fall out over your money, it makes good sense to think in terms of an independent, professional executor. Whatever you do, don't forget to tell him: he cannot be forced to act for you, and he would certainly take offense if you neglected to inform him in advance of what, in many cases, turns out to be quite an arduous duty.

An executor has no power to act until a court grants "probate" — proof that the will is valid and official authority for him to proceed. He will do his best to carry out your wishes, but remember that a will can be challenged. A surviving husband or wife, an unmarried daughter, a son under twenty-one, and any children who cannot maintain themselves because of mental or physical disability can ask for reasonable provision to be made out of the estate.

EXPENSE ACCOUNT

An arrangement designed to exploit human weakness for the benefit of the firm. The theory is simple: a bottle of champagne, a portion or two of caviar followed by Mignon de Bœuf en Croûte Lutèce, a bottle of Château Lafite, and an obliging hostess in gownless evening strap are held to be more effective in capturing contracts for one's products than the quality, price, or speedy availability of the said products.

Sometimes this is actually true. But more often than not the expense account lunch, dinner, or late-night entertainment merely softens the client up for a deal which, one could argue, would be signed anyway. It is a debatable point. The Americans call expense account lunches "eating meetings," and having attended quite a number I can vouch for the fact that a good deal of important business is conducted on these occasions. (Americans are much too obsessed with business to discuss anything else.) The Japanese, on the other hand, use expense accounts to finance the kind of binge which would be quite impossible on their salaries. I once announced, to a group of Japanese businessmen in Tokyo, that I would be interested in seeing the Ginza — Tokyo's nightclub district. Immediately, half a dozen volunteered to show me around. I took it to be an acknowledgment of my importance, but as the evening wore on I realized that I was simply an excuse. We went to a hideously expensive geisha party, at which my hosts delighted in crawling about on all fours, and playing pat-a-cake and musical chairs — with sabutan cushions substituted for seats. We had a lot of fun, but business was never mentioned.

In Britain, expense account living is less frantic, but certainly qualifies as a tradition. An expense account is less of a status symbol than it used to be, but still confers a certain distinction. Some companies are more widely known for their parties than for their products. And some executives command the affectionate respect of their colleagues for their ingenuity in devising acceptable returns. The Labour Government of 1964–1970 made a determined effort to clamp down on what, in their prejudiced wisdom, ministers dubbed "grouse moor living." It did so by changing the rules under which all expenses were tax deductible; henceforth, it said, most of a firm's entertainment would have to be paid for out of a firm's profits. It made life a little more difficult for junior executives, but expense account living at the top went on as before. British traditions are hard to destroy, and expense accounts go back to Sir Francis Drake, whose account books, itemizing his expenses in the year of the Armada, came up for auction at Christie's not long ago.

The same, of course, is true of the United States, where George Washington set a splendid example during the War of Independence. American author Marvin Kitman, who wrote a book about it, says The Man Who Could Never Tell a Lie collected nearly half a million dollars' expenses for routing the British. He used "42 basic principles of expense account writing," including many still used today. Washington's fundamental principle, says Mr. Kitman, was "be specific on the smaller expenditures and vaguer on the large ones. Describe in some depth the purchase of a ball of twine, but casually throw in the line 'dinner for one army.' He also favored the 'escalation principle' — each entry should be higher than the former." Washington's skill on the financial battlefield naturally makes one wonder why he fought us at all. Could it have been just for the money? Inevitably, too, Mr. Kitman's revelations raise profound questions about other leaders. What did Napoleon's accountants say to him when he came back from Moscow, or Rommel's after El Alamein? Who signs Mao's chits?

F

FACTORING
A financial service developed in the United States, and later adopted by Britain and others. It makes cash available to a client in exchange for his book debts. As soon as a factoring company's client dispatches his products, or provides a service, to his customer, the "factor" will immediately make cash available against the invoice value of those products or services. A factor thus becomes the credit control depart-

ment, looking after debtor accounts, bookkeeping and collection, as well as providing a source of working capital in relation to the size of debts outstanding.

Many firms who use a factor regard the service element as more important than the provision of finance. The factoring company is often the only readily available financial adviser apart from the banks, and so a "family doctor" relationship develops.

It works even better where bank managers and factors work together for mutual clients; nowadays, the banks themselves are so closely involved with factoring that this is not at all difficult to achieve. The annual cost is based on the amount of work involved, the client's industry, product or service, and quality of customers. True factoring companies offer something called a "nonrecourse system of payments," which in plain English means they have no recall on their clients if they cannot obtain payment from the customers. Or, putting it another way, they accept the credit risk.

FEASIBILITY STUDY

Trying to find out if something will work. A lot of business ideas sound absolutely splendid in theory, but turn out to be duds once you start putting them into practice. A feasibility study really amounts to doing a bit of homework before you charge off in this or that direction. You look at the market and try to assess what it will bear; you estimate the cost of launching and development; you try to work out the long-term prospects. I have done quite a number of these exercises myself and to an enthusiast like me they usually prove to be a rather depressing experience. I realize, though, that they have spared me from making some very costly mistakes. Feasibility studies are nowadays regarded as an essential preliminary to any venture, and rightly so. The chief danger is that accountants, lawyers, and others may argue you out of what is really quite a sound idea. When all is said and done, business is bound to involve some risk. Homework, however thorough, can only take you so far. If you haven't the courage to go a step further you might as well join the vast army of people whose main qualification is that they know what *not* to do.

FEATHERBEDDING

Term used in labor relations to describe union rules which deliberately create, and maintain, artificial conditions. Strong unions may, for example, insist on certain flat rates of pay for certain specified jobs, regardless of whether more efficient machinery has shortened the time required to perform them. Or the unions may insist that more workers be assigned to a given task than necessary. Featherbedding is common in Britain, where labor unions have always been particularly strong. In the United States, the term is often applied in the railroad industry.

FED (THE)

"The Fed" is short for the Federal Reserve System, the central bank of the United States established in 1913. The Banking Act of 1935 describes it as a "public institution" — but it is not a formal branch of government nor a presidential agency. The system is made up of a board of governors, an advisory council, twelve federal reserve banks (representing the twelve federal reserve districts), and member banks. All national banks are members; state banks can choose whether they want to be or not. The Federal Reserve Board supervises banking activity, and has final authority over discount rates (corresponding to the British bank rate) and other interest rates. It also has power to regulate the supply of credit. In short, although it may not be a branch of the official government, it exercises considerable influence over public policy. This, of course, is true of most central banks.

The Fed's governors pride themselves on their independence and there are times when they and the administration appear to be pulling in opposite directions. A traditional complaint of all central bankers is that politicians encourage too much public spending and inflation, and that they are too slow in taking corrective measures, such as higher taxes. The orthodox banking answer is to restrict credit and raise interest rates, and this may sometimes lead to open clashes with the president of the day. In 1965, for example, William McChesney Martin, a man of decided views, challenged President Johnson's cheap money policy by raising the discount rate from 4 to $4\frac{1}{2}$ per cent. The success of this kind of thing depends almost as much on the personal standing of the man who heads the board of governors as on the authority of the Fed itself. But presidents do tend to have the last word: it is they who appoint and reappoint him. (See also MONETARY POLICY.)

FILL OR KILL
Term used mainly in commodity trading. Also called a "quickie," it is an order which limits the risk: the trader sets his own price, and if the order can't be filled immediately at the price it is canceled. (See also LIMIT ORDER.)

FINANCIAL INCENTIVE
"If you're not in business for fun or profit," says Robert Townsend in *Up the Organization*, "what are you doing here?" A good question, and one which most people ask

themselves long before they have made their first million. The answer is, perhaps, less simple than is generally assumed. The profit motive is, unquestionably, a most powerful driving force. A million (or even a few hundred thousand) may not be the most important thing in the world, but it certainly helps to make life more pleasant. Money, someone once said, "is the only substance which can keep a cold world from nicknaming a citizen 'Hey you!'" But the financial incentive argument should not be overdone. Management experts will tell you that "job satisfaction" is often more important than differences in financial rewards. Prestige, power, security, honors — and yes, fun! — are far more potent influences than we tend to acknowledge. If it were not so, most millionaires would either retire or move to the Bahamas. Even fear can be more potent than financial reward; it's remarkable how often the threat of dismissal galvanizes an executive into action.

Tax cuts are frequently urged upon governments because, it is claimed, a little encouragement to make more money will make everyone work harder than ever before. It is an attractive theory, but I have always suspected that it is more effective as a political slogan than as an economic weapon. This is partly because the majority work to live, rather than live to work. But there is more to it than that. There is no evidence, either in Britain or America, that tax cuts alone lead to a really significant change in attitude toward work. They stimulate spending, but do not necessarily stimulate effort. One economic research organization found that, on the contrary, really ambitious people work harder under high taxation. They are determined to get the things they want, and if it takes more effort to acquire the necessary spending money they will do their best. Experience also shows that, as far as industry is concerned, the general economic outlook and the availability of credit can be at least as important as tax considerations.

FISCAL POLICY
See MONETARY POLICY.

FIXED PARITY
The price officially set for a country's paper currency. Under the system created at Bretton Woods every currency had a fixed relationship with the dollar, which in turn was linked to gold. Exchange rates were pegged at levels which were adjustable only when it became clear that circumstances had made them unrealistic. This, it was argued, insured the people knew where they stood, and helped world trade. More recent developments have cast doubt on the value of this arrangement; many people consider it too rigid. (See also FLOATING.)

FIXED PRICE CONTRACT
An arrangement under which someone agrees to supply goods at a stated price. Considerable time may elapse between the ordering of, say, heavy machinery and its actual delivery. The customer would naturally like to be sure that it won't cost more than the figure originally quoted. He may, therefore, ask for a written guarantee, and if the supplier badly needs the business (as has been true of so many heavy equipment firms in recent years) he will oblige. But with costs, particularly wage costs, escalating all the time, it is a risky business. Even a modest increase may wipe out all the profit; and in the case of contracts to deliver in two or three years' time, the deal may actually result in a loss. Most manufacturers, therefore, try to build a clause into contracts which permits them to pass on unavoidable increases in production costs. (See ESCALATOR CLAUSE.)

FLIGHT FROM MONEY
What tends to happen in periods of rapid inflation, when people find that money buys less and less. The basic rules of the antimoney game are splendidly simple. One, don't hold on to money — spend it. It will be worth less tomorrow. Two, don't just leave your money in the bank, or in old-fashioned stocking-type investments. They also lose value. Three, look for more dynamic outlets — and borrow as much as you can in order to help finance what you are doing.

Like me, you probably wish you had a little more money to fly away from. For people like us the number-one rule is to buy a house on borrowed money. The value of most properties in central locations has risen enormously over the years. I have no doubt that, if you choose wisely, even today's prices will seem low ten years from now. If you already own a house, a second home, in the country or at the seaside, may prove a good investment. The better-off go in for a wide range of antimoney devices, including speculation in commodities and investment in agricultural land. Paintings and antiques have a large and enthusiastic following, and some people invest in coins, rare books, Oriental rugs, silver, porcelain — anything which is likely to keep its value better than paper money. (See TIMES-SOTHEBY INDEX.)

FLOATING
Letting the price of currency be determined by the laws of supply and demand. The international monetary system set up at Bretton Woods during the Second World War provided for exchange rates to be fixed at internationally agreed levels. (See FIXED PARITY.) Stability, it was argued, would help world trade. It did. Economists, however, dis-

liked the sacrifices which frequently had to be made in terms of economic growth for the sake of maintaining fixed rates. Britain, for example, was repeatedly forced to slam on the brakes in order to "defend the pound." Floating was said to provide more flexibility. Canada floated its dollar in 1950 as a "temporary" expedient and stuck with it for more than a decade. In 1971, President Nixon initiated a move which, within weeks, led to the widespread floating of currencies. In most cases, rates were not completely free-moving. They were simply allowed to fluctuate by much more — 3 or even 5 per cent — on either side of the agreed parity. This is known as a "controlled float," and experience suggests that it is, in many ways, better than a system of rigidly maintained rates. Britain floated the pound in the summer of 1972, but promised to return to fixed rates "as soon as possible."

FLOOR BROKER

Wall Street's term for someone who actually does the buying and selling on the stock exchange floor — as opposed to the customers' broker, who deals directly with the public outside. The word "floor" is used in Britain, too, but you are more likely to be told that your favorite broker is "in the House." The London system differs from Wall Street's in that it has both brokers and jobbers — the latter being traders who actually make the market in the shares, buying and selling them from brokers. Like all middlemen, they make their profit out of the difference between the price at which they buy the shares and the price they sell them at. Brokers have to be fast on their feet; jobbers get around less, but have to think twice as quickly. Both are generally referred to as "dealers." On Wall Street, the nearest thing to a jobber is the "specialist" — a broker who confines his activities to a group of stocks sold at one trading post. Wall Street also has the so-called odd-lot dealer and the "two-dollar broker." Stocks are dealt in on the stock exchange in units of 100 shares; anything less (i.e., anything from one to ninety-nine shares) amounts to an "odd lot." The odd-lot dealer performs a kind of wholesale function by breaking up round lots of stocks into smaller packages. The client pays the normal price for the stock, and normal broker's commission, but also has to pay a fee to the odd-lot dealer for his services. The two-dollar broker is one who makes his living by transacting business for other brokers on the floor of the stock exchange; he used to get two-dollar fees for every order carried out.

FORWARD PURCHASE

Goods or shares are often "brought forward" when sizable amounts are involved; this means the supplier undertakes to provide a stated quantity at a certain future date for a stated price. Such dealings may also be known as "futures" or "options." In the foreign exchange market, forward dealings usually involve companies that want to protect themselves against exchange risks, such as the devaluation of a currency. A company which has a large contract to buy, say, a piece of machinery from Germany may enter an arrangement which insures that the necessary currency will be supplied on the date payment is due, at the present exchange rate.

FOUNDATION

An institution, often named after its benefactor, which finances and controls worthy causes such as universities, libraries, art galleries, and scientific research. There are lots of millionaires, but the ones who really stand out are those who have managed to set up their own foundations: they are the status symbols *par excellence* in the world of the super rich. If you endow, say, a college or university you can generally count on getting at least one doctorate in return; in Britain, you may also get a knighthood. But public gratitude and recognition need not be the only motive. Indeed, it sometimes is a minor consideration. Charitable foundations get very favorable treatment from the tax authorities, and are therefore a useful way of avoiding taxation. Among other things, they can be used to keep control of a corporation in the family. Estate duty and other taxes are frequently so high that when the principal stockholder of a company dies his family has to sell large blocks of shares — and, in doing so, relinquish voting control. This can be avoided by granting or bequeathing shares to the foundation at an early stage.

Representative Wright Patman, who led a US congressional investigation into the whole subject in the early sixties, found that foundations can also become tax-free receptacles for capital gains. The creator simply makes over property which has appreciated substantially in value. The foundation is free to sell the investment (no gains tax) and to lend the entire proceeds back to the donor at a nominal rate of interest. Alternatively, it may use the untaxed money to buy a sizable share block in some company the original donor wants to control. With this control he can raise or lower the company's dividend rate, milk its large cash funds, and otherwise rearrange things to his own benefit.

FRANCHISE
A way of making money without doing all the work. You think of a good idea, get it going, and then allow other people to have the franchise — to rent the idea from you. One

obvious first step is to protect your invention by getting a patent and registering your trademark.

A well-known example of successful franchising is America's Colonel Sanders' Kentucky Fried Chicken chain, now also popular in Europe. He started with little more than a recipe, and traveled all over the United States selling concessions to hopeful small-time businessmen.

An essential safeguard, besides registering one's trademark, is to lay down fairly strict rules about what the people who buy franchises can or cannot do. An unscrupulous — or careless — operator can easily damage one's reputation.

FREE ENTERPRISE

A system based on private ownership and minimal state interference. The government is expected to provide a broad framework of laws on property, contract, patents, and the like, but to resist the urge to plan, direct, and regulate. Adam Smith, a Scottish professor of philosophy, is widely credited with being the father of free enterprise; Karl Marx is given credit for being its most influential critic.

Smith argued that man works best in his own self-interest; therefore, he should be allowed to do just that. Out of each of us doing what is best for himself individually, common good will flow. The businessman, Smith wrote in *The Wealth of Nations*, "is led by an invisible hand to promote an end which was no part of his intention . . . by pursuing his own interest he frequently promotes that of the society more effectually than when he really intends to promote it. I have never known much good done by those who affected to trade for the public good."

Well, that was in 1776, and it must have seemed like a very refreshing change from the feudalism of the previous centuries. It still holds great appeal for most businessmen, especially in the United States. "Free" is a nice, emotional word and it is easy to believe in the virtues of a free market if things are going your way. In practice, though, we no longer have truly free enterprise.

In the nineteenth century the idea of free enterprise was increasingly attacked on the grounds that it led to exploitation of the working class. Market forces can be a cruel master. The Soviet Union and other countries turned communist; countries like Britain went in for a mixture of socialism and capitalism (see MIXED ECONOMY). Key industries were taken over, planning ceased to be a dirty word, and the market system was influenced in all sorts of ways.

The decline of free enterprise, though, also reflects at least in part the changing attitudes of businessmen themselves. They want freedom, but call for protection as soon as someone gets the better of them. They believe in self-interest, but insist on government action as soon as organized labor tries to apply the same principle. They agree that free enterprise means "standing on your own feet," but readily accept government grants and subsidies.

To many Americans, President Nixon's price and wage controls seemed like the last straw: if the home of capitalism could go in for that kind of thing, what possible future was there for the market system?

FUNDAMENTALIST
Wall Street term for analysts who like to make their investment decisions on basic facts: a company's record and current rate of profits, its competitive position within its industry, the state of the economy — in short, anything which is likely to affect its performance. The assumption is that, if you do your homework, not much can go wrong. The fundamentalist has little time for people who rely on guess-

work, or for fellow analysts who believe that the study of charts — based on the behavior of the market rather than on the basic merits of an individual company — are more likely to make you money than a fundamentalist approach. It sounds like common sense, and usually reduces one's risk. It's certainly the best policy if you are chiefly interested in long-term investment. But stock market prices are made by people, not statistics, and do not always obey the dictates of common sense. Not everyone, moreover, is in agreement about which of the various fundamentals count the most. Homework helps, but it does not guarantee a profit.

FUNDING
Turning accumulated short-term borrowings into more permanent obligations. This may be done by offering bonds (long-term IOU's with a fixed interest rate) or common stock to investors, and using the proceeds to pay off bank loans and other debts. Governments also try to "fund" their debts, usually at times when long-term interest rates are relatively low. Timing matters a good deal with this kind of operation. For companies, offers of common stock are clearly a better proposition when the economy and stock market are buoyant than when they are depressed. Bond issues, too, are very much influenced not only by the general level of interest rates, but also by the mood of the market. (See also BOND and RIGHTS ISSUE.)

FUTURES
See FORWARD PURCHASE.

G

GARNISHMENT
A legal order to an employer to deduct a certain amount of the employee's salary each payday, and send it directly to the creditor until the debt is paid. I have no idea how a word which ordinarily means "to decorate" or "to adorn" came to be associated with this rather unpleasant practice. Garnishment has, over the years, cost many Americans their jobs, wrecked marriages, and occasionally even led to suicide. Some states, notably Texas and Florida, do not allow it. And in 1970 a new Federal Wage Garnishment Restriction Law limited the amount of money which can be cut out of a debtor's salary. This was done chiefly to protect the poor. If a debtor takes home, after taxes, no more than $48 a week, and he has no other assets, he cannot be touched at all. Credit companies argue that garnishment is a necessary weapon, and that the new law is open to abuse. Young people, especially, are now much more likely to go on careless spending sprees. Perhaps so. But Texas and Florida have survived without garnishment, and so have finance companies in countries outside the United States, where the practice is regarded as an excessively harsh way of collecting debts.

GATT

Shorthand for General Agreement on Tariffs and Trade. One of the major talking shops in the free world, and an important provider of customers for Geneva hoteliers. The General Agreement was negotiated at Geneva in 1947, and is based on a number of worthy principles — nondiscrimination in trade, negotiated reductions in tariffs (customs duties), and the gradual elimination of other barriers to trade, such as restrictive government-buying policies, special export finance, or quantitative restrictions on imports. The principles are constantly discussed, and often implemented. The so-called Kennedy Round, for example, resulted in many negotiated reductions in world tariffs.

However, principles often fall foul of financial realities, and GATT rules have been flouted with impunity on more than one occasion. In 1964, for example, Britain introduced an import surcharge — prohibited under GATT regulations — and kept it going despite protests from other nations. In 1971, the United States did exactly the same. The European Common Market has developed trading agreements which, strictly speaking, are against the principles of GATT and so has Japan. The trouble with GATT is that it depends entirely on the voluntary recognition that trade wars are bad for all concerned: it can condemn, but it has no teeth. Codes of conduct tend to look good on paper, but are a great deal less impressive when they have to pass the test of actual experience.

GAZUMPING

British term for what, alas, is quite an old, established practice: breaking a gentleman's agreement (by which the British have always set such store) between someone who wants to sell his house and a prospective buyer. What happens is that, before legally binding contracts are exchanged, the seller pulls out of the deal — usually because he's had a better offer. It is, of course, possible for the other party to raise his own bid, but in many cases he simply can't afford to.

Gazumping tends to be particularly widespread at a time when houses are scarce and money is plentiful. The upsetting part, from the buyer's point of view, is not only that he loses a house on which he and his family have set their hearts, but that he has been involved in a waste of time and expense. Efforts have been made to stop this kind of thing through legislation. A simple self-help solution is to ask for a written assurance from the seller, when agreement is first reached, that he will reimburse the cheated buyer if he should subsequently refuse to sell at the agreed price.

GETTING THE COUNTRY MOVING AGAIN

No one quite knows who fathered this gem, or what it means. It has nothing to do with trains, redeployment, or emigration. Its main purpose is to cash in on the dissatisfaction of people who feel, for one reason or another, that they're in a rut. The late John F. Kennedy used it with great effect. Britain's Harold Wilson did so after him. "Getting the country moving again" is a great favorite with Convention Man, and has a number of offsprings. One of the best known is "building a new society." I'm not sure who is supposed to do the building, and what the end result is meant to look like. I do know, though, that we can do it because "ours is still a great country and we are still a great people." I know, too, that it's done by "building on the solid achievements of the past" and by "releasing the energies of the people." The solid achievements of the past do not, of course, include anything achieved during the years when one's opponents were building the new society. Once you have done the releasing, you must "get rid of the little men with small minds," and "wage war on inefficiency." The little men, needless to say, are not you and I, but the people next door. And inefficiency, as we all know, is a sin for which we can safely blame the other fellow. You deal with it by pointing out that "the world does not owe us a living." A good platform speech is one which includes half a dozen or more of such phrases: they have the inestimable virtue that no one could possibly disagree with them.

GLAMOUR STOCKS

Also known as "high fliers," "go-go stocks," and "market swingers." Anything, in fact, that is likely to appeal to speculators eager for quick profits. They are often linked to fashions in whole industries: at one time it was atomic power, then electronics, then aerospace. Or they may be stocks in fast-growing corporations run by particularly able and audacious individuals. Or they may simply be stocks which benefit from the well-publicized success of some other better-known company; some professionals call these "blue chippies."

Behind these glamour stocks, as my good friend Eliot Janeway put it so well in *What Shall I Do with My Money?*, are the "cats and dogs," the junk. "When the ferryboat comes into the dock," says Eliot, "it brings garbage in its wake. There are stock peddlers who, seeing U.S. Steel go up 20 per cent, look around for a peripheral steel mill that can be sent shooting up even further. There have been little nickel stocks that have shot up by 300 to 400 per cent . . . Stocks of under-financed and over-publicised franchise operations, together with garage laboratories whose names ended in '-onics,' were the highest-flying junk in the American markets before the whistle blew for the great reckoning."

Need one say more?

GLOBOCRAT
A fellow who can run his company's operations anywhere in the world. Like a diplomat, he may have two years in Africa, two years in England, and another two in France, teaching the natives how to apply American business techniques. The well-trained globocrat tends to be more successful than the home-based executive who drops in for a week or two, partly because he is more sensitive to local customs and partly because he has more time to assess business prospects. With the growth of giant corporations, operating in many different countries, the number of globocrats is likely to rise sharply in the years to come.

GNOMES OF ZÜRICH
Swiss bankers. The name first found its way into the newspaper headlines when British Labour ministers used it during the sterling crisis of 1964. The Gnomes were held to be cruel, heartless, vindictive men, determined to destroy all socialists. Cold and heartless they may be, but no more so than any other group of bankers. They deal in money, not emotions. The term was, in fact, quickly extended to cover all Continental banking firms which, in the course of their work, have occasion to deal in currencies. The labeled firms made convenient bogeymen. The Gnomes themselves took it all with remarkably good humor. I went to Zürich, Basle, and Geneva several times during the years 1964 through 1967 to make films for BBC television. The bankers I interviewed were not in the least offended by their nickname; indeed, some were rather proud of it. Nearly all

made the valid point that it wasn't their job to project the value of a currency, but the government's. They insisted, moreover, that the real Gnomes were in London, a bigger financial center than Switzerland. British money institutions and commercial firms, they said, were the biggest speculators of all.

The name "Gnomes of Zürich" has, in recent years, also been heard in connection with speculative attacks on the dollar. Zürich's answer applies as much to the United States as it does to Britain. (See also NUMBERED ACCOUNT and SPECULATOR.)

GOING PUBLIC

Selling stock in a privately owned business to the general public. This is often done to raise money for expansion; if the company has good prospects, going public may be preferable to borrowing heavily from a bank. Another motive is to raise cash for one's personal use. A businessman whose capital is tied up in, say, a chain of restaurants may be attracted by the idea of unlocking part of it at a good price. A third reason is to get a stock market listing, and to be able to buy up other businesses by offering their owners stock which they can either keep or sell at any given time without much difficulty.

The first step, in going public, is usually to consult an investment banker. If he is satisfied that the company is sound and has good growth potential, he will underwrite the stock — that is, buy it from the owner and sell it to the public. People who have built up their own businesses usually like to retain 51 per cent, because that way they can keep control. The minority holders do, however, have certain rights and can usually count on help in looking after them.

GOLD

A soft industrially unimportant metal which costs money to keep (it earns no interest and has to be guarded) and has no intrinsic value. A gold bar doesn't even *look* pretty. You can wind a strip of gold around your loved one's finger, but a sparkling diamond will do at least as well. Your dentist can shove a chunk of gold into your mouth to fill a tooth, but it's not half as good as a nice, healthy, wholesome tooth. A piece of cheese would be more valuable if you were stranded on a desert island. And if you tried to pay your gas bill with a gold nugget you would almost certainly be prosecuted. Hoarding gold is illegal.

William Jennings Bryan, who sought the presidency of the United States in 1896, 1900, and 1908, urged his fellow countrymen not to "crucify mankind upon a cross of gold." Henry Ford called gold the most useless thing in the world. G. K. Chesterton said that "the golden age only comes to men when they have, if only for a moment, forgotten gold."

I heartily agree. Gold is not worth the slaughter and misery it has caused over the centuries, and the passions which it still arouses today. The gold rushes of the last century, glamorized by films and television, claimed countless victims. Winston Churchill's ill-advised decision to tie the value of our money to gold bullion in 1925 had much to do with the depression which developed in the thirties. Gold belongs to the past, not the future. It's a totally inappropriate symbol for the space age. To their credit the Americans, who have a vast amount of gold buried in holes like Fort Knox, are trying hard to escape the yellow peril.

As long as people continue to distrust paper currencies, the mystique of gold is unlikely to disappear. But one would like to think that, by the end of the century, its power will be broken. We shall still be attracted by its aesthetic appeal, and future generations will proudly accept gold watches and fountain pens on retirement. With luck, though, we shall learn to ask one simple astonished question: "Gold — who *needs* it?"

GROSS DOMESTIC FIXED CAPITAL FORMATION

The total amount spent on replacing or adding to buildings, vehicles, plant, machinery, and so on. Spending on maintenance and repairs is excluded. It's one of the more obvious measures of a country's progress, and therefore forms an important part of economic study. It's also one of the more mysterious, and therefore impressive, pieces of economic jargon. Don't let it frighten you: it's much simpler than it looks.

GROSS NATIONAL PRODUCT

The chief object of worship in so-called materialistic societies, most of whose citizens don't have a clue what it means. In official economic jargon, it's "the total value at current or constant prices of the annual flow of goods and services becoming available to a country for consumption and maintaining or adding to its material wealth." Roughly translated, this means that it's the way economists like to measure material progress. If you want to equate it with the life of an individual, you'd say the GNP is the yardstick by which you tell how much you have done to secure a decent standard of living for yourself and your family, how far you have succeeded in providing for services like schools and hospitals, and how much you have done to gain a reasonably secure future. In recent years, "economic growth" has become a more fashionable phrase. There has also been a tendency, in countries with a higher GNP than ours, to cast doubt on the sense of turning it into a modern god. In Japan, for example, some people scathingly refer to it as "Gross National Pollution." (See THE QUALITY OF LIFE.) In Britain, the GNP has never enjoyed quite the same status as elsewhere. This is partly because many people prefer leisure to material wealth — a preference which infuriates economists but is not difficult to defend on humane grounds. Young people, in particular, despise the GNP. The truth, as economists like to say, "lies somewhere in between."

GROUP OF TEN

Also known, more informally, as the "Paris Club." Perhaps the most important forum for discussing changes in the international monetary system, because its members are the finance ministers and top treasury officials of the ten "richest" nations in the free world — the United States, Britain, West Germany, France, Italy, Japan, the Netherlands, Canada, Belgium, and Sweden. Switzerland is not officially a member but usually takes part in the group's lending operations.

The Group of Ten has no real structure or staff, and is therefore less unwieldy than, say, the International Monetary Fund. Meetings can be called as and when the need arises, and the group has demonstrated its effectiveness on a number of occasions. It has, for example, fixed up mammoth loans for Britain, and taken the key decisions leading to the creation of "paper gold." Because it is a highly political forum, however, disagreements can be frequent — and heated. The French, in particular, frequently clash with the Americans and, to a lesser extent, the Germans and the British. Members are fond of accusing each other of being "obstinate" or "selfish" — meaning the other fellow is just as unwilling to make concessions as you are.

GROWTH STOCKS
Shares in companies whose earnings — and assets — are increasing rapidly; for many investors, it is the highest of all accolades. Companies whose shares are rated in this way often pay out very little in dividends, preferring to plow back as big a percentage of profits as possible so that they can continue their rapid rate of growth. The rate of return offered at any given price is almost invariably low. Growth stocks suit people who are more interested in capital gain than immediate income. But beware: the label is so sought-after that exaggerated and misleading claims are often made on what, before long, turns out to be a disappointingly brief period of advance. (See also GLAMOUR STOCKS.)

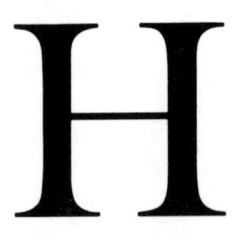

H

HARD CURRENCY
One which is freely exchangeable in world markets, and which has a comparatively stable value. Gold used to be

the principal "hard currency" — it probably explains the tag — and in many places it still is. Among paper currencies, the dollar has long been the market leader. If you go to Moscow or Leningrad, you will find that the big hotels all have shops in which one can buy goods not available in Russian stores, providing one has hard currency. Prices are usually expressed in dollars — which, according to the Kremlin, also happen to be the hated symbol of capitalism. When I was last in Moscow, a Russian friend told me the story of a Soviet couple from Kiev who walked into one of these shops, delighted with the unexpected array of goodies, and produced their Russian roubles. "Roubles," they were curtly told, "are no good. You must have dollars." The husband looked puzzled, and then asked: "And where can I get these dollars?"

Inevitably, there is a black market in hard currency. (The rouble, you will have gathered, does not qualify for this exalted status.) In Leningrad, I was twice stopped in the street by young men who asked if I could sell them pounds, marks, or dollars. They offered more than double the rate available in the hotels. That's the great thing about hard currencies: everyone wants them. Duty-free shops at many airports insist on payment in money other than their own; governments use this method to secure the currency needed to buy weapons made in, say, the United States. Many countries, including Britain and the United States, do not allow their citizens to hoard gold and some put stiff restrictions on the import and export of foreign paper currency. Travelers from hard-currency countries should take care not to exchange too much of their own money; they may have difficulty changing whatever is left over at the end of their trip into dollars, pounds, or German marks.

HATE SESSION
Therapeutic exercise designed to vent anger against (a) colleagues and (b) the boss. Dangerous if conducted in the company of apparently like-minded people. You can't rely on their discretion: indeed, they may encourage you solely in the hope of using what you say against you. Some people find it both easier and safer to shout at secretaries and wives, beat children, and kick the dog. Others take pretty young girls out to dinner and confess that "my boss doesn't understand me." In Japan, some companies have the good sense to recognize that boss-hatred is entirely natural. They provide employees with punching bags which have the boss's face painted on them: a good thump tends to save an awful lot of trouble. If you don't happen to have a punching bag handy, try hitting a golf ball. All it takes is a little imagination.

HEAD AND SHOULDERS
One of several terms used by chartists — stock market technicians who try to help investors time their buying and selling with the help of carefully kept charts. Their basic argument is that all the factors which can affect the price of a stock are already built into the price, so that there is no need to bother about factors like a company's assets, sales, or profits. The best way to spot the trend, they maintain, is to plot price movements.

Chartists were for many years regarded as a lunatic fringe, and some analysts still have no time for them. But their methods often work. Chartism is heavily laced with jargon, but you should at least be able to recognize some of the terms. "Head and shoulders" describes the pattern traced by the share price at the ending of a bull market and presages a decline. "Reversed head and shoulders" indicates the possibility of a rise in the share price. A "triangle" happens when the extreme fluctuations in the price of a share get smaller and smaller as time goes on, so that when they are marked on the chart they take on the shape of a triangle. Once the price bursts out of this triangle it is taken as a buy signal (when the price moves out above the level of the triangle) or a sell signal (when it moves off below the level of the triangle). "Double Tops and Bottoms" are points of resistance at which a share can rise or fall sharply. They represent, in fact, prices at which investors no longer wish to buy or sell the particular share. With the absence of buyers at a double top the natural result is for the share price to fall. The opposite applies to a double bottom.

Other formations include "flags," "pennants," and "saucers." If you are interested in taking up chartism, get in touch with one of the many technical services which airmail ready-to-use charts, for one stock or hundreds, to subscribers every week.

HEADHUNTER
The perfect middleman, or so it's said. He's a consultant (the business world has so many consultants that one sometimes wonders who does the buying and selling) and his job is to bring employer and talented employee together. You want a brilliant sales manager? Right, contact a headhunter. A new chief accountant? The headhunter will know where to get one. That, at least, is the theory. Armed with a list of your requirements, he will try to lure suitable candidates either by advertising the job without mentioning names — or by making a direct, but discreet, approach to someone working for a rival firm.

The headhunter, clearly, has to be a good judge of men

and a skillful diplomat. Both employers and candidates are apt to tell lies. The employer may say, at the outset, that he wants "the very best man available — a dynamic executive." If you take him at his word, and present him with an able and ambitious young fellow, his first reaction is quite likely to be one of horror: how could anyone expect him to hire someone who, in five or ten years' time, might very well try to take away his job? What he *really* wants is someone who looks and sounds like a dynamo, but who is unlikely to provide any serious competition. The candidate, for his part, will naturally attempt to sell himself as vigorously as possible — and that, as a rule, means he will offer his own, highly individual interpretation of the truth.

The headhunter has to be good at reading between the lines. But that's not all: he usually needs to know a few rather nasty tricks of his own. He may, for example, parade a few unattractive applicants before his client in order to make another man seem appealing. The bad candidate will, in all probability, never guess that he is being used. Most successful headhunters will tell you that the best people, by and large, are the ones who do not apply. They do not need the job that's offered, and in many cases prove reluctant even to consider switching. If they are good, the challenge tends to prove irresistible. Moral: if you meet a headhunter, play hard to get. But not too hard.

HEDGING
Protecting yourself against market risks. There are several different forms of hedging, but they are all based on the same principle — it pays to insure. The housewife is hedging if she stocks up with, say, baked beans because she fears an early rise in prices. A businessman may hedge by securing rights to commodities or foreign exchange ahead of

the date when he actually needs them. Stock market speculators may hedge by taking out options or spreading their money over totally different fields. In times of economic uncertainty, for example, gold or gold shares often prove to be a popular hedge. There are countless refinements to this game, but beware of getting too eager: there's always a danger that you will wind up with what is known in the business as a Mongolian hedge — an investment so well insured that both profit and loss are impossible, with at least part of your capital swallowed up by insurance premiums.

HOLDING COMPANY
See SUBSIDIARY.

HOT MONEY
One of the more picturesque bits of jargon, meaning short-term capital looking for the most profitable — or secure — home. "Hot" because, unlike money invested in plant and equipment, it can leave a country as quickly as it comes in. Banks, large industrial companies, and others have a certain amount of liquid capital available at any given time, and some of this may either be held in foreign currencies (especially if their price is likely to be pushed up by revaluation) or deposited with a bank or other institution in the country concerned. Hot money inflows can give a substantial boost to a country's gold and foreign currency reserves, but governments and central bankers dislike hot money because it tends to make for artificial situations. It's happened to Britain more than once. Attracted by high interest rates, hot money has come into London in vast amounts, giving an impression of great economic and financial strength. The outflow, however, has tended to be just as

swift — touched off by a cut in interest rates, a bad set of trade figures, or simply the emergence of a more attractive home elsewhere. The country, lulled into a false sense of security by the apparently impressive size of its short-term assets, is suddenly faced with a crisis. From time to time measures are taken to discourage hot money flows: a favorite device, used by Britain in 1971, is to ban the payment of interest on new deposits by nonresidents.

HYPERINFLATION

"Hyper" comes from the Greek, and means "over, above, exceeding, excessive." Used in this particular context, it means inflation which has got out of control. A more widely used term is "runaway inflation." Journalists sometimes claim that Britain has experienced just this in recent years, but that's an exaggeration. The most obvious example is Germany's experience in the 1920s, and again in the period immediately following the Second World War. Inflation reached such a stage that paper money was, effectively, replaced as currency by cigarettes and chocolate, and the value of savings fell to nothing. It explains why Germans, to this day, fear inflation more than anything else.

INCOMES POLICY

An attempt to influence prices, wages, and the level of employment by getting people to cooperate in a planned program, rather than leaving everything to market forces. It sounds fine in theory and is a subject of endless speculation among economists. If only workers would realize that a free-for-all in wages leads, in the end, to higher unemployment . . . if only people would accept that the answer to inflation is joint effort . . . if only employers would realize that, if workers are to exercise restraint, companies must keep down prices . . .

A prices and incomes policy has been tried in many countries. Sweden was one of the pioneers. In Britain, Harold Macmillan's government set up a National Incomes Commission, but the whole enterprise came to nothing because of the traditional class division between workers and employers.

The 1964–1970 Labour Government seemed, at first, to be more successful. Both sides of industry signed a "declaration of intent," and the Government set up a National Board for Prices and Incomes with the specific assignment of examining particular cases of prices and incomes behavior and deciding whether they were in the national interest or not. Much publicity was given to splendid-sounding "productivity agreements." In the end, though, the Government destroyed its case by constantly slamming on the brakes (and, in the process, raising prices through increases in taxes) in order to defend the pound. The public began to feel cheated, and labor unions stepped up their efforts to get more money because, they claimed, price controls had failed.

When the Conservative Government won power in 1970, it promptly abolished the Prices and Incomes Board, and reaffirmed its faith in free market forces. This policy led, predictably, to high unemployment and a slowing down in the pace of inflation. But some ministers quickly recognized that, in a modern capitalist economy, cooperation is the only politically acceptable course of action. It may be more awkward, and certainly causes more argument, but it is also more just. Ironically, President Nixon recognized the need for a prices and incomes policy just as Britain, which had tried so hard to make it work, decided to play it down. Elaborate machinery was set up to operate it. I was in the United States at the time, and it all looked so familiar — the angry letters to newspapers and politicians, the arguments on TV, the charges of cheating, the protest marches with slogans like "freeze the war, not wages." There were councils and commissions — but, as we've had cause to find out in Britain, they do not by themselves add up to an effective incomes policy. Wages apart, how do you control prices in four million rental units? How can a seven-man price commission decide what is a fair profit, and what isn't, and how can it enforce its rulings?

Incomes policies will continue to fascinate economists — and governments — for many years to come. They are not the perfect answer to inflation, or to unemployment, but they are certainly more sophisticated than the more traditional weapon — fear. I doubt if they will ever prove 100 per cent successful. They certainly won't work if politics and deep-rooted class hatred have too strong a hold. But they are a major economic weapon and will continue to be studied and applied — with the seriousness they deserve.

INFLATION
A fall in the value of money due to rising prices — or, as someone once said, the equivalent of looking at your savings through the wrong end of a telescope.

The two main types are cost-push inflation, meaning that rising costs are the chief driving force, and demand-pull inflation, meaning that too much money is chasing too few goods. A modest degree of inflation is held to be a good thing, but runaway inflation is a menace. It represents the greatest threat to our individual and collective prosperity. If this is not always realized it is because, on the surface, inflation has many attractions. A worker who secures an increase in wages automatically assumes he has bettered himself. He recognizes that the result is likely to be passed on to his firm's customers, in the form of higher prices, but consoles himself with the thought that this is none of his business. What happens, of course, is that the firm's price increase makes another worker, in another industry, ask for more money on the grounds that the cost of living has gone up. If he gets it, and that firm puts up its prices, the chap who started it all will ask for another increase on the grounds that the cost of living has gone up. And so on, and so on. This rather superficial impression of progress is also seen on a national scale. It is relatively easy to make people feel, in periods of inflation, that everything is going splendidly. Economists who warn of the dangers tend to be dismissed as Jeremiahs who are always wrong. Politicians, as a rule, go along with the public mood, because it pays them to do so. In the end, of course, comes the reckoning.

The country which fears inflation most is Germany. Twice in this century the Germans have had periods when money lost value so fast that the whole money-exchange system broke down. People were broke with lots of money in their pockets — and it wasn't funny. Just after the last world war, barter more or less replaced coins and bits of paper. Confidence in them broke down so completely that the country went, in effect, onto the "chocolate standard." Chocolate bars, packs of cigarettes, and cans of coffee were the generally accepted medium of exchange. They passed from hand to hand, just as paper money had done before. I happened to be there at the time and I well remember the reverence in which I — a young boy — held a chocolate bar. It never occurred to me that it had originally been made for eating: in my eyes, it was money.

INFRASTRUCTURE
The services which form the basis of a modern economy — power stations, roads and railways, education, and so on. Private enterprise has played an important role in the creation of many infrastructures; British investors, for example, financed much of the railway development in South America. But nowadays state finance tends to play a much bigger role. Underdeveloped countries (or, as most prefer to be called, developing countries) are suspicious of what they regard as foreign exploitation.

In both India and South America I have been told by ministers that they would rather make slower progress than have American or British companies take over. They will readily give contracts to foreign firms, and accept aid and loans from other countries, but they are determined to keep control of each operation. In many cases, existing foreign investment has been nationalized — a fact which, inevitably, has scared off potential new investors. An American or British firm will, nowadays, be reluctant to invest big money in a country like India unless it can count on getting its money back within, say, five years. This means even less foreign investment. Left-wing or nationalist governments do not seem much bothered by all this: they look more concerned with appearances than with results. It would, very often, make much more sense to welcome foreign firms, let them build large factories, and then take them over.

Perhaps the worst feature of this whole business of creating infrastructures is that it generally means some sacrifice of individual liberty and effort. Stalin, for example, held back production of consumer goods (and punished those who didn't like his strategy) because he felt that the task of building up basic industries deserved priority. Some people say that, in effect, he "wrote off" a whole generation. Future generations should benefit, but the morality of this sort of thing is obviously debatable.

IN-PLANT FEEDING SITUATION
Canteen lunch. The jargoneers have even taken over this apparently simple and straightforward part of the business scene. A recent survey of canteen lunches produced not only the above gem, but also "corporate feeding plan" and "total environmental conceptual thinking" — which, in plain English, means that the present type of works canteen may soon be replaced by leisure centers offering not only food, but also discotheques, supermarkets, and Ping-Pong.

INSIDE INFORMATION

One of the most dangerous things in the money world. There's an old Wall Street saying: "The surest way to lose money is to have a fat bank account and some inside information." Like all such sayings it's an exaggeration but contains a sizable element of truth. Investors frequently go overboard for inside information, to their subsequent regret. They are so impressed by the source that they don't pause to consider why the news should have been leaked, or to evaluate what they've been told. Unscrupulous insiders, or people close to them, sometimes trade on the gullibility of greedy speculators in quite a shameless (and often illegal) way. They may, for example, know of some impending development, such as the loss of a large contract or a sharp downturn in profits, which is certain to hit the market price of the stock. So they spread word that *good* news is on the way, dump their stock on the market, and watch the poor dumb outsiders buy it up. If they are found out, of course, they are in trouble. But there are many ways of covering one's tracks.

Even if the information is passed on in good faith, it may not necessarily be a way to easy money. Insiders often overrate the likely effect of some particular piece of news on the stock market: because it's so important to them they think it must be equally important to everyone else.

Don't get me wrong. I am not saying that inside information is always useless: my point is that it should *at all times* be treated with caution. This goes as much for news about the activities of stock market insiders as information leaked by company executives. Wall Street has developed a number of inside techniques, designed to measure the speculative operations of specialists. A close watch is also kept on the so-called insiders' reports which chronicle how much of a company's stock is bought or sold by any company officer, director, or owner of 10 per cent or more of the firm's stock. Some of these methods may be helpful, especially in the hands of an expert, but all are wrong at times, sometimes painfully wrong. (See also TIPSTER.)

INSPIRATIONAL DISSATISFACTION

An absolute must, we are told, if you want to develop PMA — a Positive Mental Attitude. You simply won't get anywhere, the theory goes, unless you are dissatisfied — wholesomely dissatisfied. The trick is to turn it to your advantage. To do this, says Jack Lacy, who runs "sales clinics" for the National Sales Executives Clubs, you "push the hot button."

How do you find the button? "Well, "you must discover what a person wants — and how you can help him to get it. The first thing you must do is to help him to crystallize a need in his mind for something he doesn't have. Then you show him that you have the best thing to fill that need. And when his desire becomes a burning desire, the person's hot button has been pushed."

It helps, apparently, to have a problem. Every adversity, we are assured, has the seed of a greater benefit. A guilt feeling is also useful: "it even motivates persons of the highest moral standards to worthwhile thought and action." Indeed, failure is considered an essential prerequisite to success and the greatest misfortune which can befall anyone is to have gone through life without encountering any problems.

I don't know about you, but I'm glad to say I'm not too badly off on this score. Why, then, am I not rich like so many authors of "inspirational" books? The reason, I suspect, is that I do not always obey all the rules. W. Clement

Stone and Napoleon Hill, the authors of a book called *Success Through a Positive Mental Attitude*, say one of the most important things to remember is always to "add something more." This amounts to adding the extra bit others have missed. For example, there was once a songwriter who wrote a song but couldn't get it published. George M. Cohan bought it and added the three little words: "Hip, hip, hooray!" The extra bit made him a fortune.

INSTITUTIONS

Insurance companies, pension funds, investment trusts, mutual funds, and other financial establishments. There are still individuals who count for a great deal, but the big institutions are now far more important than any single personality, however wealthy. Apart from their influence on the market, they exercise enormous power over industry through their voting rights. The one time when this power is clearly seen to operate is during a take-over fight. On more normal occasions institutions prefer to work behind the scenes; public clashes, it is reasoned, are undignified and expensive.

Some institutional managers would rather sell a company's stock than get involved in its problems. But getting out has become increasingly difficult, chiefly because institutions are so much more heavily committed to individual companies. There is, today, a much greater willingness than before to stay put and do something about a bad situation. "Obviously," says the investment manager of one of the biggest insurance groups, "we try to step in at a fairly early stage. Most of industry is nowadays run by managers, rather than the old-style owners, and an institutional shareholder can usually play a decisive role in any boardroom battle. As a rule, it's enough to go and see a company board, and to make certain suggestions. If they are obstinate, and insist on making a public issue out of it, we always sit down and reconsider our position. If we can sell, we may try to do so. If not, we have to decide whether to risk an open clash. Fortunately, it doesn't often come to that."

INTERLOCKING
An arrangement, often complex, which ties various associated business interests closely together — without making it necessarily apparent to the outside world. In Japan, for example, it is quite normal for the voting capital in companies to be held mainly by their commercial banks, by their suppliers, and by their clients. They all own each other. They also sit on each other's board of directors. In other words, it is a kind of commercial Mafia. Apart from the question of public interest (is it really healthy to have such underhand links?) there is the point, often made by economists, that interlocking can be a dangerous cardhouse. If a whole enterprise group faces adverse circumstances, it may have all sorts of serious consequences. Against this it can be argued that day-to-day business runs more smoothly if stockholdings remain stable, and if companies and banks doing business together all own substantial stakes in one another. It seems to work in Japan — but it does tend to leave minority stockholders out in the cold. My main objection to interlocking is that it tends to be surrounded by too much secrecy.

INTERNATIONAL MONETARY FUND
A special agency of the United Nations, set up by forty-five countries after the Second World War with the aim of preventing a recurrence of the disastrous events of the thirties,

when competitive devaluations and trade restrictions led to a slump in world trade. The fund became the guardian of the free world's monetary system, and its articles of agreement provided an important framework of rules for exchange rates, balance-of-payments policies, and other key factors. Each member contributed a quota of gold and its own currency, and this formed a pool from which the fund made medium-term loans to countries with balance-of-payments difficulties. It meant, in effect, that countries with temporary problems had an alternative to drastic measures which could harm the general level of international trade.

During the sixties, Britain repeatedly borrowed huge sums from the fund, in order to defend the prevailing parity of the pound. The fund's managing director, Pierre-Paul Schweitzer, was dubbed "Britain's bank manager," but he described himself as "just a hired hand." Real power, he pointed out, lay with the finance ministers who put up the money.

INVESTMENT CLUB
A group, usually friends, neighbors, or office colleagues, which meets periodically to discuss the stock market and make investments. Investment clubs are popular on both sides of the Atlantic, partly because they offer a chance to get together socially and partly because it doesn't take a fortune to join in. Clubs generally collect small sums of money from their members every month, and as a rule reinvest dividends and capital gains rather than sharing out the cash. It's reckoned to be more fun that way — and having fun is, more often than not, the main objective. Some clubs are more speculative-minded than others, and senior members usually have their own pet theories and pet stocks.

If you want to start a club of your own, it may be a good

idea to write to the National Association of Investment Clubs in Detroit. It has developed a set of rules for guidance in organizing and running a club and will be able to offer all kinds of useful advice.

INVISIBLES

Payments by individuals or firms of one country to those of another which do not involve the physical movement of goods across frontiers. They include earnings from banking, shipping, insurance, commodity markets, civil aviation, interest on overseas investments, and travel. The performance of a British play on Broadway, the shipping of foreign goods in a British ship, advice given to foreign clients, royalties paid to the Beatles, buying of British industrial know-how by a foreign firm — all these things earn money which is no less important to our overall balance-of-payments position than exports of washing machines or bicycles. The City of London, obviously, plays a key role in this field. But invisibles also include profits remitted from factories that British firms have set up abroad in order to jump tariff barriers or to satisfy the nationalist feelings of foreign governments. When this happens, the UK parent often stops direct exports — to the detriment of our published trade figures. But we are, in effect, still earning foreign exchange from its efforts.

J

JOB LIAR

For once, it means just what it says — but then it's not a scientific term. The great majority of us, an occupational psychologist called Ivor Goldstein found in a 1972 survey, lie about our qualifications when job hunting. Some even invent previous jobs.

Goldstein found that only one in four applicants lies about the title of his previous job, but from there on the "discrepancies" really build up. The lying rate on salaries is prodigious — nearly 75 per cent. The average exaggeration runs around 10 per cent but some embellish their earnings by anything up to 25 per cent. On length of time in the previous job, the average person will extend this by six months or more. But it's not unusual for an extra year or year and a half to be added on.

Goldstein says some employers are getting worried enough about these "exaggerations" to take them into account when making appointments, and to increase checks. Liars, beware.

K

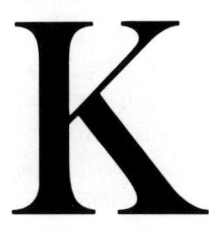

KARAT SCALE
A way of defining the amount of other metal — often silver — alloyed with gold. (Because pure gold is too soft and liable to wear to be used extensively in jewelry, it is generally alloyed with other metals.) Pure gold is 24 karat. In the United States jewelery is usually 10 (in other words, just over 40 per cent pure gold), 14, or 18 karat; if you can afford to shop at Tiffany's, you will also find 22-karat jewelery. In Britain the lowest standard accepted is 9 karat (which accounts for more than three quarters of the gold trade), with the range extending through 14, 18, and 22 karat. In America the popularity of fraternity pins and other award emblems accounts for a vast production of 10-karat alloys. In both countries, careful watch is kept on all gold production, and every article is stamped with a mark guaranteeing the declared gold content. Unlike the British, however, American producers are allowed a leeway of half a karat either way.

KENNEDY ROUND
One of the more enlightened periods of haggling over tariffs on international trade which take place, from time to time,

in Geneva, Switzerland. It was, in essence, an attempt to speed up reductions by replacing bargaining over rates on individual commodities by general cuts on most or all of them. The United States and the Common Market confronted each other for the first time, but altogether fifty-three countries took part. The debate was tough and exhausting, but in the end it was agreed to cut tariffs throughout the Western world by an average of 27 per cent. The Kennedy Round was generally seen as a decisive defeat for protectionism.

KEYNES

John Maynard Keynes (1883–1946) was the most influential economist of his generation and possibly of this century. Educated at Eton and King's College, Cambridge, he was a brilliant student in mathematics, politics, and philosophy. He eventually turned to economics in order to prepare for a civil service examination, and in 1906 entered the India Office. Two years later Keynes accepted a lectureship in economics at Cambridge, and during the First World War he did important work in the treasury department. The result was a highly successful book, *The Economic Consequences of the Peace*. His biggest impact, however, came with the publication of his *General Theory of Employment, Interest, and Money* in 1930.

The timing could not have been better: after the Great Depression, economic theorists were in disarray and desperately needed a savior. Keynes adopted basic premises a little closer to reality than those of his predecessors. He argued against laissez faire, and made a strong case for government intervention to compensate for the uncontrollable vagaries of private capitalism, even if it meant governmental deficits. He advocated a permanent policy of keeping interest rates low, and put heavy emphasis on the need to maintain full employment. His theories were by no means universally accepted, but his policy suggestions were practical enough (as well as correctly timed) to be widely adopted by politicians in desperate search of solutions. Keynes gave economics a new lease on life, and his views still command a very wide following today — although, inevitably, some of his arguments are increasingly challenged. Keynes was a skillful writer, but his *General Theory* is hard going for any layman. No matter; what counts is his ideas had, and still have, practical value. Keynes was not only a brilliant thinker; he also proved himself a highly successful stock market speculator. You can't ask for much more, can you? (See also PUMP PRIMING.)

L

LAISSEZ FAIRE
Literally "let do," a French phrase used by economists to sum up the classical doctrine that the market always knows best. Supporters of laissez faire argue that the free pursuit by individuals of their own interests is likely to produce the greatest amount of wealth for a nation. State interference is not only unnecessary, but positively bad. The doctrine had a particularly strong hold in the nineteenth century — and

that, as far as I'm concerned, is where it belongs. Even Mr. Heath's government, with its much-publicized demand that people should "stand on their own two feet," accepts that it is out of date. It's generally recognized that the government has a right — indeed, a duty — to direct the use of resources in the interest of the community and to use the tax system to insure a fair distribution of income. If unemployment reaches a socially unacceptable level, ministers cannot shrug their shoulders and say that free market forces must be allowed to take their course. If they do, they soon find themselves out of office. Even in the United States, the home of capitalism, laissez faire has been rejected by the Nixon administration, which took the unusual step, in 1971, of announcing machinery for controlling the level of wages and prices.

LEADERS INDEX

An index produced by the Department of Commerce based on the movement of twelve "leading" business indicators. They are called "leaders" because they normally move up and down ahead of the whole economy. Economists watch the index carefully for signs of a change in trend. A recession, for example, may be signaled several months in advance by a flattening out of the index or an actual drop. By the same token, a sustained rise heralds a recovery for the economy in general. Some economists, and many businessmen, are skeptical about the reliability of the leaders index and prefer to wait until they have confirmation from other barometers, such as capital spending. And just try to tell a man who is out of work that he has no need to worry, the index is going up. He'll tell you what you can do with your index. But as barometers go, it is quite useful and keeping an eye on it (the index is charted on the front page of the

Wall Street Journal as each new monthly figure is released) is one of the easier ways of becoming your own economist.

LEAKS

Disclosures of information by means other than an official statement. Often, but not always, unintentional. A financial journalist may hear that a particular company is to get a massive, highly profitable new government contract. The official who has leaked the information frequently does not realize its potential value. Or he falls into traps set by ingenious, scoop-hungry reporters. Most financial leaks center on take-over bids. A lot of people tend to be taken into the chairman's confidence once an approach has been made. They include directors, accountants, outside advisers — and, inevitably, their wives. The temptation to gossip, or even to make money out of the situation, is always strong.

There are many other types of leaks — some designed to blacken reputations, some to influence decisions that are about to be made, some to affect share prices during a take-over fight, and some to let the public know what a great guy the leaker is. Leakmanship is a much more popular art than is generally realized. In the newspaper business a leak is more commonly known — and praised — as a "scoop." And the biggest, if not the most expert, leakers of all can be found in the government. Ministers constantly leak information to the press. They talk "off the record," which means the stuff can be used as long as you don't say who told you — a device which enables the government to issue a denial if the leak proves embarrassing. Occasionally they also tell you things which are "for background only" — not for repetition, which is the official equivalent of "strictly between you and me." One advantage of this particular form of leakmanship is that ministers can "test public opinion" without actually committing themselves to a certain course of action. It is also a way of applying pressure on, say, a foreign power without making a public statement.

LEASING

One of the more interesting branches of finance — it means the renting out of all types of plant and equipment. Many firms find it more convenient to lease equipment rather than tie up capital in expensive fixed assets. They can do so by going to a finance company or bank, many of which undertake just about every conceivable type of operation, from leasing oak casks for whiskey maturing to leasing aircraft. Some specialize in tailoring their leases to fit particular requirements, especially for large contracts. They can equip complete factories, leasing everything down to typists' chairs.

Don't confuse leasing with short-term hire or contract hire, or rental provided by suppliers and manufacturers of such items as light commercial vehicles, earth-moving equipment, accounting machines, computers, and the like. A leasing agreement is usually divided into two periods, primary and secondary. The total period can be as long as ten years. The primary period varies from three to seven years; during this period, the rental reflects the value of the equipment, and if for any reason you should want to cancel the deal, you will have to allow for rentals still unpaid. The secondary period can also be from three to seven years. Rentals are nominal and termination can take place without the need for further payment; the period can be extended at will.

Since leasing is a financial operation the lessee is usually responsible for maintenance, insurance, and all running costs.

LEVERAGE
The relationship between a company's common stock and so-called prior charge capital. The latter includes anything with a prior claim on the year's profits and assets — notably bonds and preferred stock. If there's a high proportion of it, the company is said to have a "high leverage." The significance of this for investors is that high leverage increases the likelihood of fluctuations in dividends on common stock. In good years, when profits show a healthy rise, the part available for common stockholders jumps smartly. In bad years, when profits fall, the amount left over for them drops sharply and the dividend may be reduced. Many investors dislike companies with high leverage and stay clear of them. It's certainly a point worth watching out for if and when you are thinking of buying stock.

LIMITED PLEASURE-POSTPONING MECHANISM
What you've got if you find it hard to resist the persuasiveness of door-to-door salesmen. The phrase was fathered by Dr. Milton J. Huber, associate professor at the Center for Consumer Affairs at the University of Wisconsin, clearly a prince among jargoneers. Dr. Huber has made a close study of the buying habits of 100 Detroit families, all of whom were overburdened with debt. The study revealed that the great majority of them had two dominant personal characteristics: they were impulsive and they had a complacent, even carefree, attitude. They admitted finding door-to-door salesmen irresistible; some said they finally refused to answer the door when a salesman rang because they knew they were too weak. Dr. Huber also found a "confusion of roles" between the married partners. Almost one half of the couples, he says, demonstrated a lack of coopera-

tive decision-making or intelligent planning. One husband expressed it this way: "We don't argue over it. If either of us wants something, we buy it."

Sound familiar?

LIMIT ORDER

One of the ways in which an investor can control the price he pays for shares. A lot of people simply ask their brokers to buy a particular stock which they think will go up. This is really a request to buy "at the market," which means the dealer will buy the number of shares asked for at the best price he can get. With a widely traded stock this is a reasonable enough approach, but in many other cases it is more sensible to give buying and selling limits.

Stock prices do sometimes change quite sharply within a matter of minutes or hours, especially if there are rumors of a take-over bid or if the shares have been strongly recommended by someone with an influential following. A limit order gives your broker flexibility. If you are buying, he must not buy at above the price you give. If you are selling, he must not sell at below the price you give. It's a lot better than telling him that, say, you want a stock you've seen recommended at $5. The chances are that other investors have also seen that tip and the price will be higher by the time your broker or bank manager, however smart he may be, gets around to carrying out your instructions. The broker or bank manager then has to go through all the trouble of contacting you and telling you that there are no shares on offer at $5 and that the price is now so much higher. Unless you are quick, the chances are that the price will be still higher by the time your new instructions are carried through. How much better all around it would have been to have said at the outset to buy at $5, or the nearest he can get to this, with a limit of such and such a figure.

LITTLE MEN WITH LITTLE MINDS
The fellow next door. The little men with little minds are people who, according to our politicians, must be disposed of as part of the "war against inefficiency." It's all part of the free enterprise philosophy and makes excellent sense to economic experts. The trouble is, however, that the little men with little minds have a vote like everyone else. And although they enthusiastically applaud the principle that everyone must learn to "stand on his own two feet," the little men do tend to get a bit difficult when it turns out that the people who propound this theory actually mean *them*.

LOAN SHARK
A creature which someone once defined as "a rapacious fish that attacks people when they are beyond their financial depth." A more orthodox definition would be "a lender who offers money at exorbitant rates of interest," but I prefer the more colorful version. The loan shark preys on people who, for one reason or another, have got themselves into a financial mess and feel desperate. They may not know how to go about raising money from a reputable loan company, or they may have foolishly damaged their credit rating. The loan shark seems a friendly enough fellow, and he often operates in deceptively plush surroundings. His customer is so glad to have found help that he doesn't bother to read the small print. He signs whatever is put in front of him, and only discovers afterward that he has committed himself to a deal which may, in the end, land him in an even bigger mess. A cardinal rule, in dealing with this kind of operator, is to do nothing without legal advice. But this is not easy to tell people who are in bad trouble. (See also USURY.)

LONG-TERM
A convenient phrase if one wants to explain why an investment has turned sour. When critics howl for your head because, say, a stock you have recommended drops by 50 per cent, you calmly point out that you advised them to "buy for the long-term." This can be anything up to sixty years — by which time you will probably all be dead.

The money world has many other devices for hedging one's bets, or passing the buck. There's no need, for example, to commit yourself to embarrassingly precise market forecasts. You can say that the market is likely to "move sideways," or that it is "bound to fluctuate a good deal during the coming months." You can suggest that this is "a tricky period for forecasting, perhaps more tricky than usual," and go on to say that "we are, perhaps, approaching a turning point." You can urge investors to "watch out for opportunities to pick up bargains," or to be "highly selective," without actually telling them where the bargains are, or what to select. If things go wrong, you can blame shakeouts, speculative excesses, and "technical factors."

LOSS LEADER
Retailer's term for goods deliberately sold at a loss in order to attract customers. Bread and sugar are often used as loss leaders. They are essentials, and price-conscious housewives tend to be attracted by notices which offer them at an obviously favorable price. Supermarkets are particularly fond of using this technique, because they know that, once inside, the customer is likely to buy a lot of other goods on which they make a bigger profit. Manufacturers of goods with well-known brand names don't like the practice, because it tends to undermine the whole price structure.

LOWER SOCIO-ECONOMIC STRATA
Working class. It sounds much more acceptable, doesn't it?

M

MACROECONOMICS
See MICROECONOMICS.

MALTHUSIAN DOCTRINE
Named after a clergyman called Thomas Robert Malthus, who began to worry about the population explosion long before any of today's worriers were born. His *Essay on the Principle of Population*, published anonymously in 1798, caused a heated controversy. He devoted the next five years to further study of the subject, and in 1803 brought out a new edition much longer than the original, this time under his own name. The Malthusian doctrine is simple: unchecked breeding of man causes the population to grow by geometrical progression, whereas the food supply cannot grow so rapidly.

"I think," wrote Malthus, "I may fairly make two postulates. First, that food is necessary to the existence of man. Secondly, that the passion between the sexes is necessary, and will remain nearly in its present state." Man, he suggested, could apply the remedy by prudence and self-restraint, just as he could avoid illness due to gluttony or drunkenness. He advocated late marriage, which he maintained would be good for human character and for the institution. Everyone should resolve to have no more children than he could support. This moral code, he felt, should be reinforced by society, through the simple expedient of refusing charity or public support to any families which could not support themselves. It seemed a harsh prescription for a clergyman to advocate, but Malthus justified it on the grounds that it was the only humanitarian remedy in its ultimate effect, shortsighted benevolence being a palliative which could only make the situation worse. It was Malthus's doctrine, and his solutions, which first earned economics the label "dismal science." His forecasts have failed to come true in the Western world, largely because of substantial increases in agricultural and industrial productivity which he did not foresee. But Malthus has had a considerable effect on economic and social thinking, and many economists still echo his views today.

MARGINAL ANALYSIS

To the economist, "margin" is a term meaning "extra" or "last." A large and complex network of theories has been built around the significance, or alleged significance, of that marginal or last product, worker, land, capital, or purchase.

The most popular example (generations of economics students have struggled with it) concerns the behavior of consumers. The consumer, so the argument runs, allocates income in order to derive the most satisfaction from the whole of it. His buying behavior, though, is determined not by the average satisfaction he gets but from his satisfaction in buying an additional or a marginal item.

The general assumption is that the value of anything to the purchaser declines as he acquires more of it. A hungry man would pay a great deal for one loaf of bread. A second loaf would give him less satisfaction; therefore it would be worth less to him. Presumably he would go on buying loaves until he reached a point where the cost of paying the price demanded would cause him more pain than the pleasure he would get from eating a loaf. The last loaf he buys — the marginal loaf — therefore determines the extent of his demand.

This kind of theorizing clearly offers scope for all kinds of fascinating refinements. One can postulate, abstract, induce, calculate. One can draw graphs, build models, construct hypotheses. One can write whole books about it. But how relevant is it all to the real world, as we know it? Do people really make such elaborate judgments? Do *you* draw up charts to determine the last unit of each product you would buy at a given price? Or do you act on impulse, follow fashion, listen to the advice of wives, husbands, or friends? How far are you influenced by advertisements and attractive packaging? Do you think the buying habits of a man (or woman) of sixty-five are the same as they were when he or she was twenty-three?

Theorists reply that they are only trying to determine general trends, and that their deductions are better than guesswork. Perhaps so — as long as they don't lead to wrong decisions. (See also ECONOMIC MAN and MODEL.)

MARGIN BUYING

A method, popular on Wall Street, which allows you to buy stocks without putting down the full purchase price. The "margin," in this case, is the amount you put down as a deposit. The rest is financed by the broker, who charges interest on the loan. Margin buying has obvious appeal to people who like to speculate, and was one of the chief factors behind the great crash of 1929. At the time, money was easily borrowed and you could secure ownership of a stock by putting down 10 per cent of the purchase price or even less. A lot of people margined themselves up to the hilt, and were ruined when the whole deck of cards collapsed. Ever since, the Federal Reserve Board has had the power to decide what percentage deposit has to be paid to the broker: it has varied from 50 per cent to the full 100 per cent. The idea, clearly, is to prevent excessive speculation. But there are other deterrents. Interest rates, for example, often tend to be so high that the game isn't worthwhile unless you can afford to deal in very large amounts. Another snag is that, if you have a margin account, your broker keeps the shares as collateral. It should be okay, and usually is. But brokers are not infallible, and they do manage occasionally to lose stocks — and even to go bust. An alternative to margin buying is options.

MARKET RESEARCH

Answer this question — do you like this book? If not, why not? What kind of book would you like to have bought instead? Then why on earth didn't you? When did you last beat your wife? If not, why not? What do you think of market research? Do you (a) find it a waste of time, (b) think it's the only way to sell, (c) not know what it's all about?

Market research is a boom industry because everyone is seeking reassurance drawn from the law of averages. Businessmen, politicians, advertisers, and newspaper proprietors consider it the best policy to follow the rest. They all feel they have a USP (unique selling proposition, in case you didn't know) but are afraid of setting the pace. The old-style entrepreneur is dead; the emphasis today is on scientific decision-making based on the collection and evaluation of appropriate data. Market research started with the mention of finding out who bought a particular product and why. It has since advanced to the point where products are designed to fit in with the researcher's findings. In theory, this avoids waste in producing things that won't sell, and makes it possible to direct advertising at a carefully selected audience.

In practice, market research often leads companies up the garden path. Consumers are asked what they intend to buy, regardless of whether they have given the matter serious thought and often at a time when they couldn't care less. Many people, moreover, make fun of researchers by deliberately giving phony answers. Another problem is that few people know what they really want; they are better at telling questioners what they don't like, and even then their comments may be misleading.

Market research is a useful tool, as long as it isn't taken too seriously. The scientific jargon used by researchers is impressive enough. The results, as a rule, are less so.

MARX

Karl Marx (1818–1883) was a German socialist, economist, and sociologist who devoted his life to destroying the capitalist system — on paper. His prose was turgid and many of his ideas were impractical, but he must certainly be counted as one of the most influential economists of all time. Marx developed his theories against a background of high unemployment, low wages, long hours, and deplorable working conditions, and it isn't difficult to see why he detested a system which produced such blatant injustice. Marx himself lived in dire poverty for most of his life and when he died not more than eight people attended his funeral.

The basic point of his long and involved arguments was

that the capitalist system could not by its very nature survive; that it carried the seeds of its destruction. This reasoning was based chiefly on the view that life is one long class struggle, that workers lack the power to demand a greater share in the new wealth created by capitalism, and that the proletariat in industrialized societies (Marx was thinking primarily of countries like Britain and Germany) would eventually rise and seize power from the ruling class.

Despite superficial appearances to the contrary, most of his predictions have turned out to be wrong. The proletariat has not carried out a socialist revolution in any highly industrialized state; what now goes by the name of communism has won its victories chiefly in backward agricultural regions. The proletariat has not maintained a united front and the system has not destroyed itself, mainly because it has shown a far greater capacity to adapt than Marx thought possible. He did not foresee the growing power of labor unions, the impact of democracy, and the possibility of progress through evolution. The working class has not suffered increasing misery, but has enjoyed, in most industrial nations, a rising standard of living. If Marx could spend a week in some of the American and European suburbs, he would be astonished. Most of the benefits promised labor as a result of "dictatorship of the proletariat," such as the eight-hour day and social insurance, have become fact. Indeed we have gone further than the *Communist Manifesto* envisaged, and this progress has been achieved with the active support of the middle class.

It won't do, though, to dismiss Marx merely because his forecasts contained historical errors. He did have a major impact on social development in large parts of the world, and one is certainly entitled to ask how far his teachings — and the events they inspired — helped to produce the infinitely better conditions we take for granted in the Western world today. (See also FREE ENTERPRISE.)

MATRIX ORGANIZATION
See PROJECT MANAGEMENT.

MATURITY
Nothing to do with growing up; it means the date on which a loan is due to be repaid, or a life insurance policy becomes payable. It may mature in five years' time, or have five years to maturity. In this sense, it's like a good wine —except that loans rarely get any better with time.

MEDIA GROUP HEAD
One of the countless titles which advertising men bestow upon themselves to impress us with their importance. "Media" means newspapers, magazines, television, cinema, posters — anything which provides a platform for the adman's talents. "Group" means more than one account. "Head" can mean anything an adman wants it to mean, but generally signifies that he's in charge of something. Taken together, the three words certainly look more impressive than, say, "executive in charge of baked beans accounts."

Other titles you may come across include "Account Executive" (the fellow who is supposed to look after your interests, but somehow never seems to be around when you want him); "Assistant Account Executive" (a trainee who does all the work); "Copywriter" (usually a frustrated novelist who has settled for writing one-line slogans because it's better paid); and "Art Director" (the chap who decides what kind of pictures should go with the slogans).

There is no good reason why an aspiring millionaire should know any of these titles — except that it *could* save him time and money.

MEMORANDA

Also called "memos." Pieces of paper in various colors (green, yellow, and white are British favorites) on which thoughts are allegedly summarized. Academic economists are reputed to write the longest memos, but civil servants are not far behind. It's the tornado of paper whirling through the corridors of power that holds the government together.

Memo-writing is an art. A good memo is a joy to behold. The brilliant colors of the paper, the neatly typed rows of scintillating bureaucratic prose, the tiny elegant initials of the author — these are things which cannot possibly be replaced by a soulless phone call. It is not only their appearance which makes memos so important. They are also an invaluable substitute for decisions. Decision-making is always an unpleasant business, liable to upset colleagues and friends. It's much nicer just to write a memo. "Should we," you ask, "do something about sludge?" The memo is fed into the pipeline, passes through the trays of twenty grateful colleagues, and with a little luck ends up on the top man's desk. He writes a memo to one of his senior advisers, who in turn will pass the memo — duly initialed — back along the line. In industry the process may be a little faster than in government, but is essentially the same.

One of the many useful functions of the memo is to show what a clever chap you are. Assume, for example, that someone in your office has a really good idea. If you're quick, you can get it down on paper before he does. By the time he gets back to his desk, your memo is already on its way to the top. If he's foolish enough to write a memo of his own, it will simply look as if he has shamelessly stolen the idea from you. Similarly, a slip by one of your rivals can be brought to the attention of the department chief by a solicitous memo offering help. "I'm sorry to hear," you tell your rival, "that your decision has produced such unfortunate results. Do let me know if I can do anything to get you out of this mess." Twenty copies, circulated to heads of departments, should do a most gratifying amount of damage.

MERCHANT BANKS

Term used to describe London's more adventurous banks; the nearest US equivalent is an investment bank. The word "merchant" comes into the term because that's what most of the men were before they became bankers. They have usually traded in all sorts of commodities and later found it more profitable to leave the actual trading to others and to deal in credit instead of goods. Most of the founders of the best-known merchant banks were descendants of seventeenth-century traders on the Continent: the Rothschilds came from Frankfurt, the Barings from Bremen, the Warburgs and Schroders from Hamburg, the Brandts from St. Petersburg, the Lazards from Alsace. Morgan Grenfell was founded in 1838 by an American called George Peabody, whose family came from St. Albans in Hertfordshire.

Most of the merchant banks are still privately owned, and they are deeply involved in industry. They finance exports (some have thriving subsidiaries in the United States) and help small firms to raise capital. They bring likeminded companies together in corporate marriages, and act on behalf of individual companies in take-over fights. Some industrialists see them as troublemakers, "thinking up deals and urging you on so that they can make a fat profit." The merchant banks themselves claim they are a uniquely British institution, superior to American investment banks in skill and in their wide range of contacts all over the world. Modesty has never been their strongest point.

MERGER
See TAKE-OVER BID.

MICROECONOMICS
One of the branches of economics; as its name implies, it is concerned with detail. Economists specializing in this area are chiefly concerned with the economic behavior of individuals and well-defined small groups of individuals. Prices play a major role in microeconomic theories. People, unfortunately, have developed an annoying habit of behaving irrationally and forecasts based on theories often turn out to be rather wide of the mark. To an academic economist, of course, this is of no great consequence — his satisfaction is largely derived from proving points on paper. Some experts, however, think that macroeconomics is more useful. "Macro" means taking a broader view; this branch is concerned with general behavior, and the economy as a whole.

MILLION
Unit of currency in daily use among government officials charged with the task of deciding how to spend our money. Also used increasingly by large corporations, whose leaders do not like to be bothered with lesser sums. Individuals who possess at least one of these units are known as millionaires, but the word means different things in different countries. It's much easier, for example, to become a dollar millionaire than a sterling millionaire — and in Italy, a million lire is less than $1,750. Journalists use the label fairly indiscriminately, to add glamour to a story that might otherwise be very dull. Few people actually have a million in the bank; real millionaires tend to be shrewd investors. They may be

worth a million, but paper values can be misleading. Stock prices can go down, as well as up, and fortunes sometimes take a nose dive overnight. If the money is tied up in plant and equipment, a millionaire may actually find himself hard up. However good these assets may look on the balance sheet, they only mean something if they produce a reasonable profit — and if it's possible to find a buyer for them at any given point. Because of this — plus the natural tendency for most people to exaggerate their personal wealth — it pays to be skeptical when you read that someone is a millionaire.

MINK

Yes, mink. Included because it's not just a fur, but part of the executive kit and an important index of wealth. The arrival of the first mink is usually taken as a sign that the owner's husband has made the transition from "other ranks" to executive class. To begin with, it is, as a rule, only a narrow strip, sheltering a restricted area from shoulder to elbow and looking as though it came from a rack marked *office furs*. Vice-presidential wives are expected to own at least one full-length model, and presidential life-companions must have two or three and reaffirm their affluence by trailing them carelessly along floors. When not in use, of course, they must be kept in cold storage.

Minks have to be earned by years of office functions, retirement cocktail parties, sports meetings, and dinner dances. It's important not to move ahead too fast: presidential wives tend to get angry if some junior executive's spouse turns up wearing one which is superior to theirs. If she happens to be younger and more attractive into the bargain, her husband's chances of promotion may be set back by ten years.

MIRACLE MEN

Journalistic shorthand for self-made Japanese tycoons like Soichiro Honda and Masaru Ibuka, of Sony. Both dislike the label. Ibuka told me, not long ago, that there were no miracles in business. "To be a success," he said, "takes a lot of hard work and effort. You have to have a good target, a good aim. You can't wait for miracles." Ibuka first recognized the commercial possibilities of transistors on a trip to the United States in 1952. He admits that the task was far more difficult than he had expected, and that "three or four times" he was tempted to give up. If it had not been for the profits earned by Sony's monopoly position in the Japanese tape recorder market, he probably would have done so. But he pressed on — and the result is one of the world's most fascinating success stories. He still works 'round the clock: "I want to do so much," he says.

Honda, who started his business in a 17-by-18-foot shack, also takes little time off. I interviewed him at the company's research institute on the outskirts of Tokyo. Honda was in overalls. He never goes near his head office: the actual running of the business is left to bankers and accountants. On the wall of his tiny reception room was a notice headed "Management Policy." It listed five points: proceed always with ambition and youthfulness; respect sound theory, develop fresh ideas, and make the most effective use of time; enjoy your work and always brighten your working atmosphere; strive constantly for a harmonious flow of work; be ever mindful of the value of research and endeavor.

Honda told me that, as a young man, he went to a technical high school and was dismissed. "I told the principal that I didn't care about diplomas: they had less value than a cinema ticket. If I had to go through my own company's entrance exam today, I wouldn't pass." Advice to others? "Simply to do what you like to do. One must be happy at work. That's the most important thing of all."

MIXED ECONOMY
One in which some parts of productive industry are owned privately and some publicly. Britain has a mixed economy: basic industries like steel, coal, and power are nationalized and subject to government direction, while most of our manufacturing industry is in private hands. This arrangement complicates economic management and means that the Government has much less power than it likes to pretend. Unions tend to have a good deal of say over the level of wages, and it is industry — not the administration — which fixes prices and decides on the level of investment in new plant and equipment. Planning and forecasting are both more difficult than they would be if we had a "controlled" economy.

MOBILITY
The degree to which labor and capital is willing and able to move elsewhere. Movement of capital is often impeded by exchange controls. Movement of labor is extensive, especially among the young, who are less weighed down by commitments than their elders. People may switch from one region to another, if a better job is available there, or from one industry to another, if the latter seems to offer better prospects. The process is, of course, made easier if employers are willing to help with housing and the like. Mobility is an important factor in economic management; it is clearly wasteful if one part of the country has a high rate of unemployment and another a serious shortage of labor.

Many people, of course, also seek jobs abroad. Canada and Australia have always been popular, but Britain's entry into the Common Market could mean considerable movement between Britain and the Continent. The Common Market rules provide for free interchange of labor, and this has already been achieved inside the Community. Work permits have gone, and things have been made much easier for workers who move across Common Market borders. There is an international vacancy clearing system, which tells workers where the most jobs are. The European worker doesn't need to have a job in another market country before he moves there: he simply packs his bags and joins the line. Once he has moved, he can take advantage of the complex system that the Community has devised to insure that the migrant worker who pays social security contributions while he is abroad accumulates the same benefits as his foreign workmates. The migrant worker has health insurance in the country where he works; if his family stays at home and needs medical treatment while he is away, the country in which he is working will pay the cost. If he becomes unemployed he will, from 1973, be able to draw unemployment benefit paid by the country where he has been working, even if he goes abroad again to look for a job in another country. Family allowances are paid at the normal rate to the worker's family — even if they stay at home — by the country where he is working.

Continental workers, of course, will have the same rights to seek jobs in Britain. It could, over the years, produce a significant change in social habits — more intermarriage, new holiday and retirement areas, and the creation of a new, genuine breed of "Europeans." But there are snags, too. Mobility is difficult for people seeking jobs in public services, and for the professional classes. Qualifications such as degrees and diplomas still mean very different things in different countries.

MODEL

A theoretical construction designed to represent, as far as possible, what happens in real life. Economists have been known to build tangible models (one made a model of the price system using a large water tank and floats) but usually they are content with paperwork. Most would prefer to make controlled experiments with actual people, but since this is difficult to arrange they make do with assembling various known influences and relationships and constructing an edifice which, they hope, comes close to reality. The treasury department, for example, uses a macroeconomic model in preparing the annual budget to estimate its probable effects on economic performance. Model building is a fascinating exercise, and many economists take enormous pleasure in it. But models which incorporate expectations (as opposed to those which are purely mechanical) often fail because people don't behave the way they are supposed to. Politicians and labor union leaders, in particular, are inclined to defy logic.

MONETARY POLICY

The use, by governments, of various methods to influence the economy through interest rates, control of banking and installment credit, and regulation of foreign money coming in and out of the country. It is one of the two main economic weapons in the hands of a government. The other is "fiscal policy," meaning the management of an economy through variations in taxes and the like. Some governments place more reliance on monetary policy than others. In difficult times, and particularly when one's currency is under pressure, there is a tendency to make use of a severe credit squeeze. One political merit is that it is, as a rule, less unpopular than straightforward increases in taxation or a wage freeze. But there is a good deal of argument, among experts, about the effectiveness of monetary policy in economic management. Most are agreed that it is wrong to place too much reliance on this side alone: ideally, it should be used in conjunction with other measures. But, of course, it's the politicians who have the last word.

MONEY
A substance known in America as "the poor man's credit card" and in Russia as "the element that makes stupidity shine." In Britain, we like to pretend that we are not very interested in money, but for all that we talk an awful lot about it.

Nowhere else — no, not even in America — do newspapers devote so much space to money affairs. And nowhere else do people get quite so involved in arguments over how much one should pay the head of state, elected leaders, business executives, doctors, and garbagemen.

We remain largely indifferent when it's a matter of how much to spend on fighter planes, troops, foreign aid, and grants and subsidies, even if the amounts involved run into hundreds of millions. Public money is a concept which, to most of us, has little meaning. But let an individual — or a group of individuals — try to procure a little extra, and we all feel qualified, indeed compelled, to pass instant judgment.

There is a basic shabbiness about all our arguments over money: a joyless, suspicious, resentful mood which makes Britain look disturbingly petty. The Americans and Germans worship success; we give the impression that we despise it.

The chief reason is, of course, that we've had appallingly little economic growth since the end of the last war. A vigorous, expansionist climate makes it possible for everyone to progress. We don't mind seeing others do well if we're doing nicely ourselves. Retrenchment, on the other hand, invariably produces ill feeling.

Not surprisingly, no one ever admits that his complaints are inspired by envy. We like to claim that our objections have a more noble base. So we talk about morality.

Some of the loudest protests against the alleged sinfulness of trying to acquire money come from those who already have more than an adequate amount of it. People are bitterly opposed on what they assert are moral grounds to pay claims, strikes, betting, welfare benefits, and other ways of making what appears to them a wholly unjustified attempt to encroach on their territory. The moral grounds, invariably, consist of the assertion that the "country is in a mess" — which, in one form or another, it always is. (If it isn't the balance of payments, it's inflation, and if it isn't inflation, it's unemployment.) Labor unions that want more money are "letting Britain down."

At the other end of what remains of our class structure, militant labor unionists and left-wing M.P.s insist that profits, dividends, inherited wealth, money made on stocks and shares, large houses, and even business expenses are fundamentally immoral.

Somewhere in the middle are the people who have neither wealth nor the labor unions' bargaining power. They are the teachers, doctors, parsons, and judges who resent the fact that status should nowadays be measured by a yardstick which clearly puts them in second or third place. Unable to keep up, they condemn "materialism" and sing the praises of poverty. "Money doesn't buy happiness," they intone. And, of course, "money is the root of all evil."

All sections seem agreed on at least one thing: even worse than the attempt to make money is the enjoyment of spending it. To enjoy money is considered vulgar and depraved; to enjoy it publicly is a sin.

Perhaps this is the real English disease?

MONEY SUPPLY

A term which, surprisingly, did not become fashionable until the late 1960s. Definitions vary, but basically the concept is meant to cover bank deposits plus notes and coins in the hands of the public.

What makes it really interesting is the argument, which began in the late 1960s, between two camps of experts. On the one side, there are those who believe in the superiority of fiscal policy (use of taxes and the like) and of interest rates in economic management. On the other, there are those who argue that both have been much overrated, and that it's no less important to concern oneself with the quantity of money which is around at any given point of time. The latter camp, of which Professor Milton Friedman of Chicago has long been the acknowledged leader, has been much helped by the fact that heavy reliance on fiscal policy and interest rates has not, in recent years, produced the results which were hoped for and confidently expected. The Friedman case, basically, is that the money supply can and should be controlled, that it has a bigger effect on total expenditure than tax changes, and that the authorities should aim at a fixed and steady growth in the quantity of money — say 5 per cent a year — and not try to chop and change in accordance with their reading of the economic barometer.

The US Treasury, the British Treasury and Bank of England, the Bank of France, and other authorities have all accepted that the professor has a valid point and, in practice, much more attention is now paid to the money supply. But everyone, including Friedman himself, is aware that his case is not, by itself, a panacea. "We are," warns Friedman, "in danger of assigning to monetary policy a larger role than it can perform, in danger of asking it to accomplish tasks that it cannot achieve, and, as a result, in danger of preventing it from making the contribution that it is capable of making. A steady rate of monetary growth at a moderate level can provide a framework under which you can have little inflation and much growth. It will not produce perfect stability, it will not produce heaven on earth. It will make an important contribution to a stable economic society."

If nothing else, Friedman's argument has led to a general awareness that fiscal policy and changes in money supply should reinforce each other and not pull in opposite directions. It may strike you as obvious — but that certainly is not how it appeared to officialdom in earlier years. (See also MONETARY POLICY.)

MONOPOLY

The control by a single seller of a commodity or service. Patents and copyrights grant a high degree of monopoly; Polaroid is perhaps a good example. Natural conditions may also produce monopoly situations: a raw material or popular product may be in such short supply that a single firm can corner the market. (The test is whether, and how far, it can affect price by withholding supply.) But such circumstances do not usually last for long. Shortages tend to be temporary, high prices encourage the development of substitutes, and antitrust legislation makes it possible to break up monopolies which become too powerful. The nearest thing to an absolute monopoly is the public ownership, in countries like Britain, of services such as gas, water, electricity, and railways. This "gas and water socialism," as it is sometimes called, is said to be necessary to insure continuity of essentials and their most economical use — an argument which, clearly, is open to debate. Labor unions, too, have increasingly come to exercise monopoly power. (See also FREE ENTERPRISE and TRUST-BUSTING.)

MONTHLY INVESTMENT PLAN
A scheme run by the New York Stock Exchange (and commonly referred to as M.I.P.) which allows the small investor to buy listed stock in fixed-dollar amounts. The deal must be initiated through a broker, but after that it's all done through the mail. The investor simply picks a stock, and sends in whatever money he can spare — though, in practice, the scheme lays down a minimum of $40. The stock is bought for him at the opening price the day after his check is received. The M.I.P. allows automatic reinvestment of dividends or other income, so that you can let your investment ride. It's a good way of letting people of limited means in on the fun. The chief difference between the M.I.P. and a mutual fund is, clearly, that one buys individual stocks rather than a stake in what, in effect, amounts to a shopping basket.

MOONLIGHTING
Having a second full- or part-time job. Skilled workers like carpenters, painters, and plumbers are particularly fond of moonlighting, but the practice is also growing among white-collar professions like accountancy. In America, not long ago, a major university discovered that one of its professors also held down a lectureship at a college several hundred miles away. He commuted between the two. The professor

lost his job, partly because he had concealed his moonlighting activities and partly because the university felt that any man in a responsible position can only do one thing satisfactorily at a time. Most industrial employers share that view. One can usually spot a moonlighter by his tendency to yawn or fall asleep at his main job. His biggest enemy, though, is not his employer (one can always get another one) but the tax collector. Concealing earnings from tax men is a risky business.

MORTGAGE

Any deal under which property or land is given as security for repayment of a loan. Mortgages are particularly useful when the purchasing power of paper money is falling — which, in practice, means nearly all the time. Say you take out a mortgage for $50,000 over twenty years. By the time it falls due to be repaid, the dollar will be worth considerably less — perhaps as much as 40 or 50 per cent less. But you are obliged to pay back only the amount originally borrowed. You will, of course, be charged interest, but the cost is tax deductible and, on balance, you should come out well on the right side. People who do not own their own homes should certainly seek as large a mortgage as possible, and for the longest possible term, from a savings institution or other source before venturing into the stock market. And unless they happen to fall on really hard times, they should firmly resist any temptation to repay it before the final date. Buying apartment buildings or other income-producing property tends to be quite complex, and should not be undertaken without professional advice. But here again, the same general principle applies.

MULTINATIONALS

One of the business catch phrases of the seventies, often said to be "the most exciting" development in modern industry. Based on the view that this is the age of the large corporation, transcending old-fashioned national boundaries. Common Market enthusiasts foresee the creation of a great many large and efficient European companies "capable of carrying out a global economic strategy." This could be achieved by, for example, promoting a merger between British, French, and German electronics companies. Such a giant, internationally owned and controlled, could unify its research and development and use the EEC as a base for "invading" world markets. It would gain the economies of scale. One argument in favor is the growing power of American giants like General Motors and IBM, who already have subsidiaries in many different countries.

The concept sounds excitingly positive, and is backed by the actual experience of existing international corporations like Royal Dutch Shell and Unilever. But there are several important obstacles, notably the fact that Europe does not yet have a unified company law. And a growing number of politicians and economists are worried about the effect the concentration of industrial power is having on the consumer. Size is no guarantee of efficiency: on the contrary, experience over the past decade suggests that it often leads to exactly the opposite. And, of course, less competition reduces choice and frequently means higher prices. The urge to merge exists, and is perhaps stronger now throughout Europe than it has ever been before. Every industrialist is aware of it; so is almost every labor union executive. But at the same time, there is considerable skepticism about the likely outcome. This is all to the good. The giant corporation, as I argued in my book *Merger Mania* is not necessarily the best solution to the problems of the seventies. Multinationals are here to stay, but there will be plenty of cause for regret if the enthusiasm is overdone.

MUNICIPAL BONDS

State and city bonds. They are used by governors and mayors to finance the cost of building roads, schools, hospitals, and other projects. They offer lower returns than government bonds but interest paid on them is totally exempt from federal income tax. If the bondholder lives in the state where the bond was issued, the interest is also exempt from state tax. Municipal bonds tend to be taken up as they are issued, generally by wealthy investors, and the market in them is nowhere near as active as in other bonds, let alone common stock. They are of no use if you want excitement.

MUTUAL FUNDS

A means of spreading one's risk when investing in stocks. At least, that's the idea. If you have limited savings and put them all into a savings account or into a government bond, you need have no fear. But most people feel the urge to do better: they are more interested in capital gain than a regular, but fixed, rate of interest. A mutual fund sells you shares in its operation, and in turn employs experts to invest the money in a wide range of business concerns. If these investments rise in value, this is reflected in the value of each share in the fund. And the fund undertakes to buy back a customer's share, at any time, for cash.

The idea is so simple, and the attractions appear so obvious, that mutual funds have enjoyed enormous popularity over the years. In the United States alone, there are more than 800 active and easily available mutual funds. They are also popular in Britain (where they are called "unit trusts") and many other countries. Many have done well for their clients, but experience has also highlighted the need for caution. One of the first lessons people tend to learn is that markets can go down as well as up. It may seem an easy enough point to grasp, but it's amazing how many newcomers think that capital gains are more or less guaranteed.

Another lesson is that mutual fund operators are not in the business for their health; their charges can be substantial and there's no certainty that their investment skill matches their flair for salesmanship. But the most important lesson is that the mutual fund concept is open to abuse. Clients' money may, for example, be used to finance reckless speculation, or to further the interests of directors rather than investors. The Securities and Exchange Commission in America and the Stock Exchange Council and Board of Trade in Britain have all kinds of regulations and try to keep a close watch on mutual fund and unit trust activities. But their efforts are not always enough — as the example of Bernard Cornfeld and the Investors' Overseas Services (IOS) demonstrated only too well.

Cornfeld made his biggest mark in a variation of the mutual fund idea called the "offshore fund." This is, basically, a means of taking large-scale advantage of tax and other financial loopholes in different countries around the world, notably places like the Bahamas, Bermuda, Panama, Liberia, Liechtenstein, and Luxembourg. Cornfeld's companies avoided the regulations of markets like Wall Street and London, but in the process also got around almost all the controls designed to prevent speculation getting out of hand. The Cornfeld empire collapsed in 1970, and although there are still plenty of offshore funds in operation, investors have developed a healthy skepticism toward this type of venture.

N

NAFTA
Short for "North Atlantic Free Trade Area," a scheme proposed in the sixties as an alternative to British membership in the Common Market. The idea was that Britain and the United States should join together in a separate club. NAFTA had several prominent supporters on both sides of the Atlantic, but failed to make much impact where it counts — at the top.

Lyndon Johnson poured cold water on the scheme when it was suggested to him in 1967. He was not interested in forming closer ties with us. Nor was Congress. The proposal was revised when Richard Nixon became president, but it soon transpired that he was no more enthusiastic. Britain's place, he let it be known, was in the Common Market.

NATIONAL DEBT
Frequently, and quite wrongly, said to be the amount a country owes to other countries. It is, in fact, largely the total of what successive governments have borrowed from us — the public. The major part of Britain's national debt

represents borrowing to finance government expenditure in the two world wars.

Citizens who put up the money were given government bonds in exchange. The best known of these bonds is War Loan $3\frac{1}{2}$ per cent, quoted on the stock exchange, but there are many others. Bonds which have no fixed repayment date, like War Loan, are known as "funded debt" — i.e., the debt has become permanent. Other borrowing, including treasury bills, national savings certificates, and premium bonds, is called "unfunded debt" and has to be repaid in due course. This can be done either by raising the necessary money through taxation or, more probably, through issuing new government "paper" with a different repayment date. Both in theory and in practice, the national debt can go on forever.

Occasionally, voices are raised in protest. In America, for example, the late President Eisenhower once said that "in effect we are stealing from our grandchildren in order to satisfy our desires of today." But economists pour scorn on that kind of thinking: all we are doing, they maintain, is leaving to posterity a contractual transfer and reshuffling of the national income of the time. In short, the word "debt" has acquired a new, more sophisticated (or, if you prefer, cynical) meaning. You borrow without ever intending to repay; your sons can also arrange things in such a way that the question of actual repayment does not arise.

There are, as you might expect, snags in such a philosophy. The first and most obvious is that governments find it quite easy to borrow whatever they like to finance whatever mad project may take their fancy (including wars). The second is that, although it can "roll over" the repayment of capital, the government cannot avoid paying interest. In the case of undated stocks like War Loan, of course, this can be conveniently small, but future generations of investors are unlikely to show enthusiasm for stocks which yield an insignificant return. The cost of "servicing" the national debt is, therefore, likely to grow rather than diminish. And if some of the bonds are bought by people living in other countries, the interest paid on them is bound to be a burden on the balance of payments. As long as the money raised in this way is invested in projects which show a return, such as the construction of a new dam or a steel plant, this snag does not really matter. After all, private enterprise does not have a monopoly on worthwhile ventures. But if the government has nothing to show for its expenditure, the debt is indeed a charge on future generations — though much less, in pure financial terms, than is generally believed. The two world wars are the most obvious examples. They did not produce the kind of return that looks good on a balance sheet; the question you have to ask yourself is whether they were worth it in other ways.

NATIONALIZED INDUSTRIES

Industries owned by the public. In practice, we have no claim on them of any kind. Indeed we may lose by the arrangement, because their monopoly power allows them to fix whatever level of prices is considered appropriate. Nationalization is basically a socialist concept, founded on the argument that essential services (or the "commanding heights") should be in the hands of the community or its workers — meaning the government. In Britain, electricity, steel, power, coal, railways, the principal airlines, and even the Bank of England are all owned and controlled by the state.

Perhaps the most persuasive argument in favor of nationalization is that it helps not only to safeguard public services (nationalized industries can't go bust) but can also be used to insure a certain amount of social justice. It is, for example, much easier for a government to keep down railway fares by agreeing to make good any losses than it would be if the railway system were still in private hands. Public ownership can also stimulate the economy by promoting new capital investment in plant and machinery. Not least, nationalization can be used to preserve military security: priorities can be clearly laid down, and there is minimal risk of a conflict of interests.

NEAR CASH
Assets which can be quickly turned into cash, such as treasury bills or other easily marketable securities. A business often finds itself with sizable amounts of money which are not immediately needed. The directors may decide to leave this money on current account with the company's bank, but it's often more advantageous to put it on short-term deposit, buy treasury bills, lend it to a reputable borrower, or find some other profitable employment. The important thing is that it should be safe and withdrawable at short notice — usually seven days.

NEW
A perfectly ordinary word, but one which qualifies for inclusion because it's a veteran of a thousand expert campaigns. Advertising men, politicians, economists, and of course journalists use it constantly — often to describe something which is no more new than New York or New Orleans. Presidents and prime ministers like to think that everything they do is "new." What they really mean, of course, is that it's different — and not necessarily better. Mr. Edward Heath, Britain's premier, has the proud dis-

tinction of using "new" more often in a single speech than anyone else. At the 1971 Tory Party Conference, he said "new" no less than eighteen times in under an hour. We were, he declared, living in a new world, a world where America and Russia are looking for a new place to stand, where the new voices of each nation are being heard, where new patterns of power are being established, where countries are being forced to look for new ideas and new markets. And guess what he thought we should do about it? Right first time. We had to "walk out into the light to find a new place. A new Britain in a New World."

NEW DEAL
Political catch phrase used to describe the program introduced by President Roosevelt in 1933 to deal with the Great Depression. (Later phrases, you will recall, included John F. Kennedy's "New Frontier" and Lyndon Johnson's "Great Society.") The New Deal did, for once, contain quite a lot that was actually new. The administration launched a program of industrial recovery through public works (in other words, it created jobs for the unemployed at federal expense) and insured an ample supply of cheap credit. The dollar was devalued by 40 per cent. Housing legislation provided for large-scale construction of houses with public guarantees and subsidies. Unemployment relief was regulated and enlarged. The Social Security Act introduced general social insurance. The Agricultural Adjustment Act provided for large-scale assistance to farmers.

All this not only contrasted sharply with previous economic management, but also broke many American traditions. Not surprisingly, the New Deal met with considerable opposition. By 1934, however, there was a marked upturn in business activity and today it is generally accepted that the government has a responsibility for maintaining full employment, if necessary by going into the red. This is known as — you've guessed it — the "new economics." (See also KEYNES and PUMP PRIMING.)

NIXONOMICS

Richard Nixon himself modestly called it "the most comprehensive New Economic Policy to be undertaken by this nation in four decades." Nixonomics made its debut in August 1971, and its main feature was a system of direct controls on prices and wages. The changes were agreed to in the course of one short weekend in Camp David, and completely reversed Nixon's own and his party's policies. (See INCOMES POLICY.) They were certainly an unusual weapon for a Republican president. Officials explained that Nixonomics had become necessary because the old economic theories no longer worked. Big labor, they argued, now has so much power that it can keep on winning inflationary wage increases despite the US government's strongest efforts to cool off the economy. They have a point, but economists disagree about the value of the whole enterprise. Some argue that tough government action has a major psychological effect: if businessmen and union leaders see that inflationary behavior leads to controls and other unpleasantness it will induce as much restraint as the fear of tight credit and recession. Others argue that Nixonomics has been an exercise in futility. Professor Milton Friedman, one of its most outspoken critics, says that "the controls have had a negligible effect on inflation but they have had appreciable, and adverse effects on output and productivity . . . the immediate effect was to chill the recovery then underway by introducing great uncertainty into the calculations of every businessman."

NO-LOAD FUND
A mutual fund that does not make a sales charge. No-load funds do pay management fees, but the cost is not passed directly to the customer. Instead, a cash charge is made on the assets of the fund. No-load funds ought to be more popular than funds which take a commission of 9 per cent or more as an entrance fee, but in practice the latter are both more numerous and bigger. The main reason for this, of course, is that generous commissions attract good salesmen. No-load funds do not have an ambitious sales force and therefore do not command as much attention. They nevertheless have a good following, especially among young people, because you don't need much money to get started and because most of them have a speculative flavor.

What really matters, though, is performance. The load paid in sales charges is well worth it if your investment puts up a better show. A no-load fund that loses a third of your capital is more expensive than a successful load fund that charges you 9 per cent to get in. The load, moreover, falls quite sharply as the size of the investment rises. Independent professional advice always comes down to this: never mind the sales pitch, look at the track record.

NUMBERED ACCOUNT
A device invented by the Swiss to attract bank deposits. A client is known by a number instead of his name: his real identity is, as a rule, known only to two or three top officers of each bank. He seldom gets any interest on his money, and may actually be asked to pay a modest sum for the privilege of running the account. Banks in Canada, the Lebanon, and elsewhere offer much the same facility, but no one else has developed it to quite the same extent. Swiss

banking law relating to secrecy was passed in 1934, at a time when a lot of Jewish money was beginning to leave Germany and Nazi agents were trying to discover where it was going. Swiss bankers never fail to point this out when they are attacked for providing what, in effect, amounts to an open invitation to dodge taxes.

Most numbered accounts are used by businessmen as a means of protecting themselves against the curiosity of their own governments. In Britain and America, the tax authorities can usually pry information about a customer's finances out of his bank. If all else fails, they can get an injunction ordering the bank to disclose. Not so in Switzerland: the Swiss, taking a relatively mild view of income-tax evasion, have laid down that banks are under no obligation to tell the authorities anything about their customers' accounts. Italian businessmen, who appreciate this more than most, often enter Switzerland with suitcases full of bank notes and open numbered accounts on the spot.

Besides the obvious financial advantages they offer, numbered accounts are also considered an important status symbol. If you want to open one, you simply walk into one of the banks in Zürich or Geneva, and make your intention known. The official in charge will probably try to convince you that a numbered account is not really needed, since the Swiss banking secrecy laws pertain to all accounts and, further, a numbered account may be against your country's laws. If you insist, and your credentials are in order, your wish will probably be granted. But be sure of one thing: there's no guarantee of secrecy if the prospective client has robbed a bank (which, understandably, is considered a most dreadful thing to do) or is known to have taken part in criminal fraud. This became apparent when the question of fraud was raised in the Clifford Irving case: the bank concerned readily agreed to cooperate with American and Swiss investigators.

O

ODD-LOT DEALER
SEE FLOOR BROKER.

OFFSHOOT
See SUBSIDIARY.

OPEN MARKET OPERATIONS
One of the methods used by central banks, such as the Fed, to regulate the volume of credit and influence rates. If a central bank wants to increase the amount of money in circulation, it goes into the market and buys up government bonds and treasury bills. The money it spends will increase the balances of the clearing banks (who are generally the main sellers) and this will enable them to lend even more to the public. If, on the other hand, the central bank feels the need for some restraint, it goes in for large-scale selling of securities. This mops up money, the banks reduce their advances to customers, and the public cuts back spending. Open market operations can be quite effective, but are only part of the armory available to economic managers: they're no miracle cure for real financial ills.

OPM

Shorthand for "Other People's Money." It's the surest way to acquire wealth. The Hilton Hotel chain was built up on credit, and there are countless other examples of people who have made fortunes with OPM. "Show me a millionaire," William Nickerson has been quoted as saying, "and I will show you invariably a heavy borrower."

One favorite postwar trick has been to make a share-exchange offer for a company rich in property assets and to turn these into cash immediately after acquiring control. This is how British financier Charles Clore got the Sears shoe chain for nothing. He offered stockholders the lure of quick gain by making a bid which valued the shares at considerably more than the current market level. The board of directors defended itself in vain. He secured 75 per cent acceptances, and at once started to sell hundreds of freehold shops to financial institutions, who were always on the lookout for ways of employing their huge incomes. They paid for the shops in cash — and promptly leased them back to him. Clore got, in effect, control of properties worth more than $20 million. They laid the foundation for a considerable trading empire and, inevitably, a number of other eye-catching take-over deals.

OPTIONS

A speculative device which, according to its supporters, offers absolute guaranteed limited risk, yet unlimited profit potential. There are several types of options, but the two basic ones are "call" and "put." A call option tends to be the most popular: for a fee, you buy the right to acquire a given stock at the existing price over a period which generally runs from thirty days to six months. In short, if you have reason to think that a stock will go up, you can get hold of it without actually laying out a lot of money. A typical six-month option will cost 12 to 15 per cent of the stock's price. If you've guessed wrong, your loss is limited to that amount. If you've made a good choice, you have secured a profit at a known risk. A put option works in reverse: it gives you the right to sell at the existing price at any time over the six months. A double option (also known as a "straddle") allows you to have it both ways — but the price of indecision is double that of either the call or the put.

Some people think that options are the greatest thing that ever happened to the stock exchange. They certainly appeal to the gambler that lurks inside every investor. But remember: in buying options you are not, as you are in stocks, buying an interest in a piece of property. You are gambling in a substantial price change. You have to be right about the price move. Perhaps more difficult, you have to be right about the timing of the move. After an option expires, it is worthless.

No, I don't know why they're called "put" and "call." It's one of those things which is a mystery even to the expert.

OTHER THINGS BEING EQUAL
One of the old-time greats in economics; you can generally tell whether a man is an economist by the number of times he uses this particular phrase. It's a useful way of dismissing qualifications at the start of an argument. "Other things being equal," you say, "the following should happen." There's only one snag; other things are usually *not* equal.

OUTPUT
A word which, on the surface, is self-explanatory. But "output," as used by the economist, covers more than the actual production of goods by one particular factory. It takes in all

the goods and services resulting from the economic activity of an individual, a firm, an industry, or a country. This frequently results in problems of definition. How do you rate the services of a maid, a waitress, or a bus driver? They qualify as output, but how do you measure them with any degree of accuracy? And how about the services provided by the vast and still-growing government machine? How do you define the output of a bureaucrat, policeman, teacher, judge, or politician?

Even the production of actual goods has pitfalls for statisticians. The firm or country concerned will have used raw materials, components, and services of other firms or countries. The obvious answer is to deduct them from the gross, and this is in fact what happens. The balance is called net output. Clearly, though, there is considerable scope both for errors and differences of opinion. This is why estimates for whole trades and industries should be treated with reserve — and figures for the whole country even more so.

OVERHEADS

Costs which are not directly attributable to any particular item you produce. Head office expenses are the most obvious example, but they can be almost anything — from the money you have paid for a machine, truck, or typewriter to your secretary. Because they are so hard to pin down, they have a tendency to run away with themselves, especially in good times. (See COST-CUTTING.)

OVER-THE-COUNTER MARKET

See BIG BOARD.

P

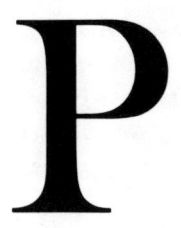

PAPER PROFITS
One of the more deceptive things in business. You may have bought a stock which is doing well, or backed a restaurateur who seems to be enjoying a great success. On paper, you show a healthy profit. But there's an old stock exchange maxim which says, quite reasonably, that paper profits don't mean a thing until you take them. The great Rothschild once said, when asked how he made his fortune, that he had done it by "always selling too soon." It may sound glib, and in a way it is. Rothschild didn't have to worry about a capital gains tax. But it's certainly a point worth bearing in mind. Paper profits are fine as long as there is little likelihood that they will vanish. Unfortunately, they often do.

PARENT COMPANY
See SUBSIDIARY.

PATENT
A legal right to make, use, or sell an invention during the period the patent remains in force — usually sixteen years. An International Convention for the Protection of Industrial Property helps to secure patent rights abroad by giving the patent-holder in a member country priority in obtaining similar patents in another country. The United States, the Soviet Union, Britain, and other European countries all belong to it.

Before an invention will be patented it must be proved to contain an element of novelty. And it won't be granted if the invention, or its use, is contrary to law or morality, or if it consists of foodstuffs or medicine with no other properties than the ingredients are already known to contain. This clearly involves some interesting questions of judgment. How novel does an idea have to be to qualify? And how does one decide, in these permissive days, how far it may be contrary to morality? No, it's no good asking the authorities; they will give neither advice nor financial assistance.

PATERNALISM
A system which claims to look after people, but which all too often means a twentieth-century form of slavery. Specially prominent in Japan. On paper, Japanese paternalism sounds very noble. There is an unwritten law that says you don't ever fire anyone. Big firms recruit young men straight from school or college and, as a rule, employ them "for life." Employers tend to talk of "adopting workers into the family," and people who change jobs two or three times in the course of their lives risk being described as "unstable characters." Luring workers away from other companies is considered bad form. If a company runs into a

bad patch, it reduces working hours and bonuses — but keeps its men. If they are inefficient, or make several bad mistakes, they are demoted rather than sacked. Fringe benefits are impressive.

On close inspection one begins to see a few snags. The benefits merely help to make up for comparatively low wages. And they tie a man down completely — which means, as a rule, that he is at the mercy of his bosses. They will expect him to put his job above all else, even to the point of working long hours overtime without reward, giving up weekends, and forgoing annual holidays. If he cannot get on with his immediate superior, life can be hell. In theory he can move, but he cannot take his accumulated benefits with him and he may be judged unreliable. So he usually stays. His career is blueprinted at the start, and seniority usually counts for more in determining salary increases and promotion than ability. At fifty-five, the company will retire him with a modest lump sum and he will get a social security pension which is seldom big enough to keep him in the life-style to which he has grown accustomed. Paternalism has contributed greatly to Japan's economic success, but many young Japanese intensely dislike it. They have already forced some changes, and more are likely to come.

PAYOLA
Slang term for money, air tickets, merchandise, and other things of value offered to disc jockeys, journalists, and anyone else in a position to publicize the alleged merits of some product or service. In the United States, plugging is comparatively easy because there are so many radio and TV stations anxious to fill up air time at the lowest possible cost. It's usually understood that, if you take part in a program

without pay, you are allowed to advertise your own product. I have done it myself, in several promotion tours for *Punch*. But payola tends to go beyond this: as a rule, it amounts to accepting bribes in order to sell something you may, or may not, believe in. In Britain and other countries where airtime tends to be rather firmly controlled, evidence of payola often means instant dismissal. The word is familiar to the British — though we also have terms of our own, such as "graft." In Italy, under-the-counter payments are known as *busterella* and in Mexico it's *mordida* — meaning "the bite."

PEACE SCARE
Headline sometimes used by journalists to frighten American businessmen. When the Vietnam peace talks started in Paris, for example, a well-known business magazine announced: "Real threat of peace in Vietnam."

Underlying this is the widely held belief that economic prosperity is difficult, if not impossible, to achieve without heavy defense spending. If you look at America's economic history since World War II, you will see that Korea and Vietnam both produced boom periods. And not only, one hastens to add, for the United States. Dozens of other countries had their economies boosted by Washington's massive war expenditure. Thailand, South Korea, the Philippines, Japan, Malaysia, and Europe all benefited enormously from America's faith in military strength.

The Paris peace talks, on the other hand, were followed by a period of widespread economic decline. In the United States itself, unemployment soared to disturbing levels. Elsewhere, governments struggled to make ends meet.

Defense spending accounts for nearly 10 per cent of America's gross national product. Whole industries are geared to war. The defense business is like no other: there is only one major customer for your output, salesmanship is not put to the test in the open market, and if you know of any engineer who can convert a shipyard into a plant making toasters or antipollution devices — well, a lot of industrialists would like to hear from you.

Given our modern, allegedly sophisticated economic management techniques, it seems absurd that peace — or the prospect of it — should cause any problems. It is indeed possible to find effective alternative ways of keeping an economy in a healthy state. The administration certainly is not short of complex plans. But there is no doubt that peace scares still make some people nervous. In the long run peace must be bullish; in the short run it tends to produce changes which are bound to hurt someone, somewhere.

PENNY STOCKS
Stocks which sell for only a dollar or two each. They are often mining or oil stocks and frequently highly speculative.

PERFECT COMPETITION
One of the many things that economists love to talk about, but which does not actually exist. It's really an analytical model of the pure form that a market would take. It involves such requirements as (1) a lot of sellers of an identical product, none able to influence the market; (2) everybody knowing exactly what goes on in this and other markets; (3) every producer's product being identical; (4) no one big enough to dominate the market; (5) no barriers to the movement of capital or workers. Need one say more? It's pure Utopia.

PERFORMANCE CONTRACT
An arrangement under which payment for a job is based on measured results for a specified task. The penalties for failure are, as a rule, carefully spelled out. Management consultants, and others offering a service rather than a product, usually work on this sort of basis. It has even been applied to schools; in the United States particularly, firms specializing in educational systems have been hired for periods of from one to four years.

A problem with many performance contracts is accurately measuring progress: it is usually a matter of opinion.

PHILIPS CURVE
Would you believe that it's a way of measuring the relationship of general changes in prices to economic activity? Well, that's exactly what it is. And yes, it was thought up by a man named Philips.

PLOWING BACK
Putting profits back into the business, instead of spending them or distributing them to stockholders as dividends. The money may be used to finance expansion, or to modernize existing plant. The process is also known as "self-financing," and is popular with ambitious and fast-growing companies. The ordinary stockholder benefits in the end, because the value of his assets is increased. Some people prefer this kind of company to one which is generous with dividends. This is because they are more interested in capital gain than income (usually for tax reasons). A high rate of profit retention, however, does not always mean faster growth. If a company is badly managed, the money may be

lost on risky ventures. Or it may simply lie in the bank, instead of being used on something worthwhile. Take-over bids, fortunately, have acted as a useful spur in these situations. A board of directors which makes a mess of things, or lacks the imagination and courage to make proper use of the stockholders' money, may well find itself the object of unwelcome attention from a more aggressive rival.

PORTFOLIO

If you own stock in one company, you are a stockholder. If you have stock in two, you are someone who is running a portfolio. Everyone who aspires to real status in the money world should have a portfolio. It makes life interesting, and offers endless opportunities for impressing other people. Supervising one's portfolio is a splendid spare-time activity, and an absorbing pastime in retirement. There are so many things you can do with it, switching from one stock to another, averaging (adding to existing stocks by a purchase of shares at a lower price), nagging your broker three times a day, writing to companies to tell them how to run your business, and talking loudly at cocktail and dinner parties about the impact of world events on your investments. If you happen to have a "go-go" portfolio, so much the better; however dull you may be as a person, it gives you an air of daring which few women can resist. Go-go stocks are those which look destined to go places; with luck, the label will also be applied to you.

PREFERRED STOCK

The name is both accurate and misleading. Preferred stockholders have a prior claim over the holders of common stock, both to dividends and repayment of capital if the company goes bust. However, preferred stocks are not as well protected as bonds and are certainly not preferred by the majority of Wall Street analysts and investors. Dividends are at a fixed rate, but are paid only out of profits. If these are not earned, stockholders tend to go dividendless or get only a part of the amount due. Most issues have a form of protection in that the dividends are cumulative; if a company's annual profits are not enough to pay the fixed rate, the entitlement is carried forward and must be paid out of any future profits.

Preferred stocks tend to give a higher return than common stocks, and therefore appeal to people who need a good income. But they do not provide a safeguard against inflation, and invariably go down in price when interest rates go up. They have had some bad spells in the last decade.

PREMIUM

Basically, the percentage above par (or face value) that a buyer may have to pay in the market for, say, a popular bond or common stock. But the word has many other applications. A new common stock may, for example, stand at a premium over its issue price (which may itself have been in excess of the par value). This may reflect the high opinion that investors have of that particular company, or may simply indicate hopes of a short-term capital gain.

The annual payment on an insurance policy is also known as a "premium." And in the property world, people taking out a lease on an apartment are often asked to pay a premium — "security-deposit." (See DISCOUNT and DOLLAR PREMIUM.)

PRESTIGE-PAY RATIO
What's it worth, in terms of sacrifice in salary, to gain the prestige which will lead to higher things? Every ambitious young businessman, if he has sense, will work out his own prestige-pay ratio. Some people settle for the best they can get right at the start, and stay put. They usually reach a certain level, after several years' service, and find they cannot move much beyond it. Others deliberately accept a low rate, and switch jobs even if it means a cut in immediate income, because the job concerned offers the kind of prestige which tends to act as a natural steppingstone. A junior-executive post in a well-known, highly successful company may, for example, be more prestigious in the long run than a high executive position in a small, run-of-the-mill firm. I have, on more than one occasion, willingly taken a sizable cut in salary because I was convinced a different job had more potential. It's a risky game, of course, and should ideally be indulged in before one runs up too many financial commitments. One must be clear, too, what kind of prestige is involved: a bigger title, no matter how good for the ego, doesn't mean much if it does not mean real advancement — both in terms of money and job satisfaction.

PRICE-EARNINGS RATIO
One of the tools investment analysts use to evaluate a stock. The p/e ratio, as it is commonly known, indicates the number of years which it would take for the stock to earn the amount of its cost. It is arrived at by dividing net earnings into the market price per share. A low p/e ratio implies an expected decline in profits; a high ratio usually means that the market thinks well of the company and looks for higher profits and, possibly, an increased dividend.

The p/e ratio is based on reported earnings, and is therefore out of date by the time it is published — sometimes by many months. It gives no indication of how safe a dividend is. Ideally, one should be able to allow for current and likely future profits, but that's difficult. In the circumstances, it's best not to place too much reliance on the p/e ratio; it's just one of the many factors to be taken into account in making up one's mind about a particular investment.

PRIME RATE
The lowest interest rate payable by borrowers with the highest credit rating. Interest rates are influenced by many facts: official policy, international trends, general business activity, and so on. The prime rate is generally regarded as both a pacesetter and barometer. Banks watch each other closely, and a change in, say, Chase Manhattan's prime rate may well touch off a chain reaction.

PRIVATE SECTOR
See PUBLIC SECTOR.

PRODUCTIVITY
What you can get out of a man — and his machine — within a given period. Anything wider usually comes under the heading of "efficiency." The term should not be, but often is, confused with production, which simply means anything which is made, moved, or provided. The productivity of labor is usually measured as output per man per

shift, hour, month, or year. In part, this clearly depends on the man himself. Labor union regulations are also a factor: in many cases, productivity is deliberately held down in order to keep more people working on a project than are really necessary. But no less an important factor is the quality of the equipment provided by the employer. The high level of productivity enjoyed for so many years by countries like the United States, Japan, and Germany owes a good deal to substantial investment in modern plant and equipment. In Britain, such investment has been notoriously low. Attempts are made, from time to time, to relate wage increases to increases in productivity. In many companies, binding productivity agreements are in force. They usually work best when both management and workers recognize the basic problems and decide to do something about them.

PROFIT
Usually defined as the difference between a company's income and outgo — an oversimplification which leaves much room for misunderstanding. Workers tend to see it as pure gain, and to equate it with "profiteering." Properly speaking, it ought not to be called profit at all, but "trading surplus." A company, after all, still has to make allowance for tax, depreciation, loan stock interest, and other unavoidable charges — items which, taken together, tend to cut the figure by more than half. Union officials, of course, are well aware of this, but it often suits them to use the word "profit" as a weapon. This is a hangover from the past, and in some ways one cannot perhaps blame them. Labor has been exploited on countless occasions, and still *is* in some cases. But anyone who takes an objective look at the overall picture will readily acknowledge that times have changed. Labor union power, among other things, has seen to that. There

certainly is no case for despising the profit *motive*: they have even come to acknowledge its value in the Soviet Union.

The most sensible yardstick, if one wants to see how a company is doing, is the return on capital employed. Add together fixed assets like plant and machinery and net current assets — the difference between the total of items like cash, outstanding debts, and work in hand and the total of current liabilities like creditors, overdrafts, taxation, and dividends. This is the capital employed. Work out how much the profit shown in the accounts comes to as a percentage of the combined figure. If it compares favorably with other companies in the field, it is a sign that the company is well managed. If you don't want to be bothered with making the calculation yourself, ask an accountant or stockbroker to do it for you. It shows you know the ropes.

PROGRESSIVE TAXATION

The principle which has, for many years, guided the American and British tax systems. Proportional taxation means that payment is made in direct proportion to income; rich and poor alike hand over, say, 20 per cent of their earnings. Progressive taxation means that the better-off not only pay higher absolute amounts, but also a bigger proportion of their income. This happens because parts of it are subject to increasing rates of tax, as in surtax and estate duty. Progressive taxation was brought in to narrow the gap between rich and poor, and liberals still argue that it is the most practical device for redistributing wealth and income. In short, it is an instrument of justice.

Conservatives tend to argue, on the other hand, that it is an unwarranted form of discrimination against the individual. They maintain that it penalizes not only the rich, but also the middle-class manager, who is the chief driving force in the economy. He cannot accumulate capital and therefore lacks the funds for independent action. "What," a nineteenth-century critic of progressive taxation asked, "would we think of a banker or grocer or any merchant who would demand for the same commodity a price varying with the wealth of the purchaser?" It is, you may feel, a fair question. But proportional taxation is unlikely to make a spectacular comeback. What we may see is more of a shift away from progressive taxes on incomes toward a so-called regressive tax system. Sales, excise, and even social security payroll taxes are regressive because rich and poor alike tend to bear the same burden.

PROJECT MANAGEMENT
Taking on particularly demanding tasks within a corporation. Also known as "task-force management," "satellite management," and "matrix organization." As a rule, it involves a temporary group of specialists from diverse disciplines working under a single manager to accomplish a fixed objective. The manager operates independently of the company's normal chain of command, negotiates directly with divisional heads for needed specialists, and is accountable for the project's ultimate success or failure. Project management has had some notable successes, particularly in top-priority US military and space programs. But despite its acclaim as yet another management miracle it has often failed to live up to its advance notices. One of the more serious problems has been open hostility between project managers and functional department heads, usually over competition for the time and talent of departmental personnel. Specialists, too, have often been reluctant to cooperate because they were being asked to take on temporary assignments with no assurance of returning to their old

jobs. In short, project management sounds great in theory but tends to be more difficult in practice because people behave like, well, people.

PROTECTIONISM
Policies designed to protect businessmen against competition from foreign rivals. High tariff walls — having the effect of making imports more expensive — are one method. Import quotas — placing a strict limit on the quantity of imports — are another. Industries such as steel and textiles have long known how to get their cases noticed in Washington. Congressmen have been lobbied. And senators anxious to please voters have been only too ready to listen.

Whether the companies concerned exercise pressure secretly or in the open, American business believes it has a good case on protection. Foreign imports threaten American jobs. The main danger is from Japan and Hong Kong, but even Europe can produce cheaper goods than American manufacturers. The US shopper likes a bargain; if foreign goods are cheaper he will buy them. Steel shows the problem at its clearest. Japan's steel industry isn't only cheap, it's also modern. It's been rebuilt using the latest techniques. And unlike America's steel industry, it has to export to live. Result: Japanese steel is highly competitive.

Successive administrations have nevertheless opposed protectionism. This is partly because there is obviously scope for retaliation. But it also reflects the understandable desire to exercise power abroad. If America shuts out the world, the world might shut out America.

PROXY
A person acting in place of another. If you hold voting stock in a company, but cannot attend a stockholders' meet-

ing, you are entitled to appoint someone else as your proxy — providing you give the company advance notice. He can vote on your behalf, even though he may not be a stockholder himself. This explains why, very often, a controversial proposal may be defeated on a show of hands, but approved by an overwhelming majority on a poll. Directors often solicit proxies in the case of, say, take-over bids. So does the opposition. American financial history, particularly, is full of colorful "proxy fights."

PUBLIC RELATIONS

A profession which, at its worst, gets in the way of understanding and, at its best, does a great deal to promote it. Journalists love to knock PR, and most of those who do so eventually end up in it. Bad public relations men spend all their time devising new letterheads, taking people to lunch, arranging meetings between busy executives who have no wish to meet, writing press releases which are meant more for the eye of the fee-paying chairman than the press, and organizing receptions at which the only noteworthy happening is that everyone present gets drunk. Good public relations men tell their employers the truth, even if it happens to be unpleasant, look after their "customers" in the press and elsewhere (internal PR is often much more important than relations with papers and magazines), and use their knowledge of human nature to produce the right kind of results.

It's a popular myth that public relations is the same thing as salesmanship; in fact, a good PR man often spends as much time trying to keep things out of the paper as putting them in. There is considerable merit in silence; as every successful businessman knows. But there's no harm in selling if the product is sound; if it isn't, however, not even the best public relations man can hide the fact in the long run.

PUBLIC SECTOR

That part of the economy which comes within the scope of the government. (By the same token, "private sector" means everything owned and controlled by individuals, private limited companies, and corporations quoted on the stock exchange.) In countries such as Britain the public sector has been greatly expanded over the last few decades, chiefly through forced governmental acquisition of existing firms. Industries like electricity, water, coal, steel, and railways were taken into public ownership many years ago. To these one has to add social services like health, education, and housing, and the local authorities. Under Mr. Harold Wilson's Labour Government of 1964–1970, ministers gradually steered away from outright nationalization — believing that the same effect could be achieved, with less fuss, by making use of the government's formidable purchasing power, encouraging mergers, providing public finance with "strings," and using ministerial influence. A scheme for capturing more of the "commanding heights of the economy" by the creation of new science-based industries never really got off the ground.

The Conservative party, which succeeded Wilson's Labour Government, believes in free enterprise and has returned some of the public sector to private investors. The Conservatives are, however, keenly aware that state ownership of key industries makes it easier to reorganize the economy, and is a useful weapon in the battle against major problems like wage inflation. Many American economists would like to see an extension of public ownership in the United States, and the country may well move further in that direction. By and large, the American businessman still clings to his traditional belief in the value of private enterprise: it's not easily shaken. (See also FREE ENTERPRISE.)

PULL

More often called "nepotism," or "undue patronage to one's relations." Pull can take many forms, but the basic requirement stays essentially the same — you must know the *right* people, "right" meaning anyone who can help your career. A man is known by his friends and contacts, and in business it is important to have influential friends. Marrying into a family firm is a recognized way of getting the first push up the business ladder, but take-over bids and mergers have tended to reduce the scope. Young businessmen who try to acquire pull through marriage sometimes find that, soon after the wedding, the firm is taken over by a bigger outfit and family connections actually prove to be a handicap. The modern managers who run large, go-ahead corporations tend to be biased against anyone who seems to owe his job to favoritism.

Push is probably more important today than pull. Push means being self-confident, or at least appearing to be self-confident, and bringing your talents to the notice of the people who run corporations or lend big money — ideally without, at the same time, offending all one's colleagues.

PUMP PRIMING

An attempt to revive a depressed economy by injecting into it more purchasing power, through government spending, than is collected in the form of taxes or other revenue. This injection requires a budget deficit — which is why pump priming is also referred to, from time to time, as "deficit spending." The government covers its deficit chiefly by borrowing, which it tends to find a lot easier than you and I do. The best-known advocate of pump priming was Lord Keynes: if you want Keynesian economics in one sentence, this is it. The basic idea is that, once the economy has been revived by public spending, an upswing in private expenditure will follow. Unemployment will fall, and the government can afford to relax again. The technique is nowadays used fairly frequently, even in conditions which fall well short of what one could call a depression. The main risk is that too much money is pumped into the economy, over too long a period of time. The combined forces of private and public spending may, eventually, produce "overheating" and serious inflation. (See also KEYNES.)

PURCHASING AGENT

The company buyer. He's usually responsible for purchasing raw materials, components, spare parts, and equipment — right down to the office stationery. A good man can save his firm a lot of money, but all too often the job goes to a pedantic type who loves to prevaricate. He delights in keeping salesmen on the hook (and, in doing so, sometimes loses the opportunity to buy at a favorable price) and he evolves elaborate procedures which make it impossible to buy, say, a typewriter without filling in a long and pointless application, and waiting at least three months for delivery. Some experts think this is because, in most organizations, the purchasing agent has a comparatively low status. He is certainly considered less important than the men who go out and sell. So he goes in for all this horseplay in order to compensate.

An exception to the rule, of course, are companies where intelligent buying is crucial — such as department stores. A top-class buyer will not only be a skillful negotiator, but will frequently be able to point out to suppliers changes in equipment or techniques which could improve the product or the service offered.

PUSH MONEY
Term for concessions made to salesmen for "pushing" certain goods or stocks. A store may want to dispose of, say, shoes that haven't moved too well in order to make room for a more successful line. The boss puts a label on the boxes saying "P.M. 50 cents," and the salesman does his best to persuade customers to buy these rather than more popular items. Wall Street, too, makes use of push money. Salesmen are offered extra incentives to dispose of certain securities, notably secondary offerings and new issues. This may make them overenthusiastic: the only answer is to check, independently, that the brokerage firm is offering good merchandise.

PUTS AND CALLS
See OPTIONS.

PYRAMIDING
A form of speculation which is possible only when you can buy stocks on margin — meaning that you put some of your own money down as a deposit, and borrow the rest from your broker at a certain rate of interest. Its popularity in the late 1920s was one of the reasons for the Great Crash. At the time, margin requirements were only 10 per cent. So, to begin with, a speculator bought, say, 100 shares of a $50 stock. He paid down $500 and borrowed the rest. The price of the stock duly went up, reaching $75. He now had a handsome paper profit, but did not cash it. Instead, his broker recognized the increased value as collateral for an even bigger loan to buy an extra number of shares. Some people carried this game to extraordinary lengths, starting

with a few hundred dollars and ending with stock literally worth millions. It worked fine when prices were rising, but often proved disastrous when they began to fall and brokers called in margins. The small-time speculator could suddenly find himself faced with the demand: "Put up $100,000 additional margin or else." He could not raise that kind of money without selling — and his selling accelerated the decline in price.

QUALITY OF LIFE (THE)

A phrase increasingly popular with countries which have achieved a high rate of economic growth. In Japan, many thoughtful people are appalled by what economic success has done to their surroundings. America's concern with the environment reflects the same kind of feeling. Their experts criticize Britain's apparent lack of drive, but also tend to envy our more leisurely way of life. There is, they say, no real virtue in hard work as such. Some people enjoy it, and no one would wish to spoil their fun. It is right that they should be properly rewarded, and they usually are. But economic achievement, as measured by the balance of payments and the gross national product, is not an end in itself, but a means to an end. And that end, it is acknowledged, ought to include leisure.

If a worker uses his extra pay to buy more leisure, he is not "wrecking the country" but simply exercising an option which ought to be granted to every civilized person. If he fights to preserve the beauty of the countryside, even though new factories would give him more prosperity, he is not being "old-fashioned and backward," but rather more sensible than people who have made economic growth their god.

There's a nice little story which I once heard in South Carolina, and which I have always felt ought to make every economist — and businessman — pause for a few seconds. It is about an African who was seated under a coconut tree resting, when he was addressed by a passing Englishman. "What," the Englishman asked, "are you doing for yourself, just idly sitting here? Why don't you get busy and develop your fields, those mines, and build cities?" "What for?" the African asked. "To establish commerce," the Englishman replied. "Commerce for what?" "So you can make lots of money." "What good is money?" "Money will bring you leisure." "What will I do with leisure?" "Then you can rest." "But why do all that," the African asked, "when I'm resting now?"

QUARTERBACK

Americans see everything in terms of football or baseball — including business. (In Britain, of course, we prefer cricket.) "Characteristically," says Harry Levinson, author of *The Exceptional Executive*, "the American executive has an image of himself as a combination coach, quarterback, linebacker and end. He designs the plays and calls the signals. He evolves strategy and manages tactics. He tackles the competition head-on, or makes brilliant broken-field marketing runs, or throws surprise product passes over the heads of the competition, or punts the economic ball safely out of danger by merger, cost-cutting, or some other emergency device. And he does it every season."

Any European planning to do business with an American would, clearly, be well advised to familiarize himself with words like "quarterback" and "punt." White House economic strategy, incidentally, is known as a "game plan."

QUOTAS

Any quantitative restriction on trade, but most commonly applied to the limitation of foreign imports. Governments use quotas to protect domestic industries from foreign competition, or to relive pressure on the balance of payments. Trade between capitalist and communist countries is mostly subject to quotas; they are fixed in direct negotiations between individual countries. Trade within the free world is not, as a rule, restricted in this way. International rules, however, allow a government to resort to quotas if there is a "serious decline in monetary reserves." The opportunity is rarely taken, partly because of the very real possibility of retaliation and partly because a large and complex system is needed to issue licenses, check abuses, and generally administer a quota system. Both Britain and the United States have preferred to make use of a surcharge — a straight percentage addition to the cost of virtually every import. The trouble with a surcharge is that firms either pass it on to customers, in the form of higher prices, or absorb it in their profit margins in the hope that it will prove temporary — a move which, of course, defeats the whole purpose of the exercise. (See also PROTECTIONISM.)

R

R AND D
Shorthand for "research and development." Obviously essential in industries in which competition is largely based on technological innovation. Computers is one example; the aircraft industry is another. America's big companies spend much more on R and D than European concerns, and the need for Europe to catch up is said to be one of the chief reasons why we need more European mergers. Studies show, however, that the fertility of innovation is not necessarily related to size. Medium-sized and large (rather than largest) firms often do best. There is an element of hit and miss in R and D; only a small share of the research results is capable of economic development. Many good ideas have come from individual inventors, rather than corporate teams; the development of Whittle's jet, for example, from an idea to a proven system cost a mere $63,000. But large expenditure greatly increases the chances of finding something worth developing — and of turning it into a marketable product.

RATIONALIZATION
Measures taken by companies, or enforced by banks or governments, to improve efficiency (profitability) by reducing the number of units of production and concentrating output in the most efficient (profitable) ones. The merger boom of recent years has generally been regarded as an essential part of a much overdue rationalization process. Many people feel, however, that the results have often been of questionable value. (See also COST-CUTTING and TAKE-OVER BID.)

RAT RACE (THE)
The relentless pursuit of success. Some people reckon the term is a gross libel on rats. Others claim that no one would ever bother to enter unless he had to. Don't you believe it. Most successful businessmen I know enjoy the rat race — as long as they are winning. They readily concede that they are missing a lot of everyday pleasures, but would hate to be out of it. Observe them on vacation — lost, ill at ease, inadequate. A business friend of mine, who I suppose merits the title King Rat, has a beautiful yacht which is moored in Cannes. But he keeps it more as a status symbol than as a provider of fun. He knows all about trade cycles, mergers, price-earnings ratios, and economies of scale — but very little about sailing. He knows how to squeeze a little extra profit out of German and Japanese customers, but he has no idea how to handle the local traders. He suspects (as all wealthy people tend to do) that everyone is going to take advantage of him the moment he gets on board. He doesn't particularly like the sea, he can't cook, and he can't speak French. Indeed, he can't do anything very much except sit on the deck and drink whiskey. Which he does for most of the day.

The beaches, each summer, are full of paunchy businessmen sipping Scotch and asking themselves, "What am I doing here?" It isn't easy to leave the rat race, even for a little while. It takes skill to do nothing, to be a bum. You can't be a frantic executive one day and a leisurely beachcomber the next: the contrast is too great. The bronzed, casual natives, who make it look so simple, have had years of practice. And they don't feel any guilt. This guilt feeling is perhaps the biggest handicap. Doing nothing strikes many businessmen as immoral. If God had meant executives to be idle, He wouldn't have given them companies. How will the office cope without them? What will the stockholders say?

Some try to get over this guilty feeling by taking files. They don't have to be about anything important; their comforting presence is enough. (It is, however, advisable not to take them along to the beach. I once saw a large, middle-aged German businessman chase a piece of paper which had, somehow, been blown out of his hands. Sweating profusely, he ran through the sand, stepping on brown motionless bodies, destroying sandcastles, and leaving small children in tears. He caught it — but by the time he returned triumphantly to his chair, several other sheets had been blown away.)

Others keep telephoning the office. "Must keep in touch," they explain happily. In countries like Spain, Portugal, and Italy, where the telephone is less than perfect, this can take up the entire day. You sit in your hotel room, staring at the telephone, waiting for the ring that will connect you with the familiar world you have so thoughtlessly abandoned.

If files have been forgotten, and the telephone is out of order, a standard ploy is to start running someone else's business. No hotel is ever run as efficiently as it should be;

no restaurant ever reaches the right level of perfection. And, of course, the proprietor is just longing to have the benefit of your advice.

For really restless tycoons, the best answer clearly is to stay at home. You'd be surprised how many do just that. "Holidays?" they ask, amazed that you should even raise the possibility that they might indulge in anything so frivolous. "I haven't got time for that kind of nonsense. A couple of days at Christmas, that's all I ever need." They love feeling indispensable, and their business is usually structured in such a way that they really are. Everything depends on the man at the top, nothing is delegated, nothing is left to chance.

The snag, of course, is that sooner or later they tend to have an enforced holiday — in the hospital. Suddenly it turns out that they are not indispensable after all; indeed, the company may actually do better. That's the trouble with the rat race: it's more suited for rats than for people.

REAL WAGES
Wages adjusted for changes in the level of prices. A lot of people judge their own personal progress strictly in terms of pay. The factory worker thinks he's better off if his pay envelope contains $10 more one week; similarly, the office worker thinks he has advanced if he is granted an "increment." They leave out of account the fact that, because of price increases, their real wages may not have risen at all.

What matters is what the dollar will buy. If its purchasing power declines by 10 per cent a year, then one needs the same sort of rise in income simply to stay in the same place. The administration has been trying to get this across to people (it is, after all, a key factor in any incomes policy) but in a great many cases the point has been neither understood nor accepted. Many people simply want to make sure that they keep pace with the cost of living — or, if possible, get ahead of it. One can't really blame them. The chief sufferers, alas, are old-age pensioners and others living on fixed incomes, because their real income has been showing a persistent and rapid decline.

RECESSION

A word which politicians love to use against their rivals; to "engineer a recession" is to let down the American people. In fact, it may mean no more than a modest reduction in economic activity. Like "boom" and "slump," the word has the inestimable merit of fitting neatly into a headline. Economists resent the journalist's urge to label everything in this way. A boom, to them, is either a peak in the business cycle or an all-out expansion of business activity which has been organized by the administration of the day in order to win the next election. A recession is somewhere in between; and a slump — which tends to follow — can be anything from a noticeable decline in economic activity, accompanied by a sharp rise in unemployment, to a period of sustained misery in which nothing ever seems to go right and which looks as if it will go on forever.

Before the Second World War, these phases recurred fairly regularly. Postwar economics, however, has succeeded in evening out fluctuations. Ups and downs have been no less frequent, but less pronounced. Politicians still like to scare us by warning that, if we don't watch our step, we shall see a return to the dreaded thirties. But voters have heard this too often to be greatly impressed: there is a general feeling that politicians "wouldn't dare." It flatters them; politicians have much less power to control events, once they are under way, than most people think.

REDEMPTION
Nothing to do with religion, but simply financial jargon for "paying back." Companies and governments don't repay, they redeem. There's no reason, it's just their policy.

REDEPLOYMENT
One of several euphemisms used to get around the politically explosive word "unemployment." Strictly speaking, it means getting people to find other jobs — an exercise also known as a "shakeout" or "releasing surplus labor." The idea is to put people into industries designated by the government of the day; in times of balance-of-payments trouble, this usually means exporting firms. It sounds good on paper, but it is difficult to apply in practice. If economic activity is low, there simply may not be enough new jobs available. Retraining facilities, too, are generally inadequate to deal with the sudden shakeout of a large number of men. The biggest snag with redeployment is that people have an irritating habit of behaving like human beings. They frequently prefer to stay where they were born, or where they have relatives, rather than take a better-paid job elsewhere.

In the Soviet Union, unemployment does not exist — at least not officially. Bourgeois decadents may caddishly point to "local reserves of labor," but the individual Russian is encouraged in his constitutional right to guaranteed employment by the absence of any unemployment-relief payments, and by a tough rule book governing industrial behavior.

The acting profession, too, does not officially acknowledge the word "unemployment." Out-of-work actors are always "resting." In recent years, a campaign has been afoot

— on both sides of the Atlantic — to get the public to accept unemployment itself as respectable. Unemployment, we have been told, should not be regarded as the evil of our age but rather as a country's reward for increased efficiency. In other words, it is actually a virtue. In Britain, several ingenious schemes have been put forward, including one which proposes that the unemployed should be paid a proper living wage — a wage for not working. Carried to its logical conclusion, this means that before long "full-time unemployed" would come to be regarded as a proper job. You could enter it in your passport and regard yourself as a highly esteemed member of the community — a man who helps his fellow citizens by keeping out of their way.

I fancy, though, that some spoilsport would sooner or later start to worry about the harmful effects which paid-for idleness might have on your soul and try to find you things to do. I'm afraid there are an awfully large number of precedents. The ancient Egyptians diverted the hordes of unoccupied *fellahin* to building the pyramids, and Hitler built the German autobahns on this same Cheops/Keynesian principle. More recently, a bird watcher from Atlanta, Georgia, stood as a write-in presidential candidate for the Front Porch Party. He ran on a ticket which proposed to put the unemployed to work boring holes in dead trees so that our feathered friends would have more convenient places to nest in.

Fortunately, there is no shortage of less strenuous pastimes. There are already quite a number of people who are unemployed in the traditional sense of the word, but not jobless. Actors, novelists, poachers, playboys, and criminals all come into this category. They would, I imagine, be first in the lines of those asking for a "living wage." As far as I can see, there would be nothing to stop your joining them. Another well-tried method would be to form a committee or association. There are already a vast number of bodies which serve no purpose other than to keep their officers busy.

Not least, you could form a nontrading company. I know several companies which ceased trading several decades ago, but still maintain boards of directors. They meet once a month, chat about the weather, collect their fees, and go home again. Making unemployment respectable clearly requires only a little imagination. Indeed, thinking up suitable schemes might itself be a way of keeping you busy.

There are, of course, people who think the whole campaign is a lot of nonsense. They insist that unemployment is contemptible, and want governments to do everything in their power to keep us all producing cars, engines, ships, and sprockets. How old-fashioned can you get?

REVOLVING CREDIT

One of the most popular forms of consumer credit; it means you can charge new purchases even if you haven't completely paid for previous ones, as long as you make regular monthly payments on the outstanding balance. To quote one leading bank's brochure: "You apply for a loan once — and thereafter for as long as you wish you will always have a preapproved line of credit to buy your cars in the future . . . and your loan is strictly confidential. In fact, you never have to come to the bank for an interview. Simply fill out this do-it-yourself auto-loan kit in the privacy of your home or office, and mail it to us."

Revolving credit accounts go by all kinds of names. Sometimes they are called "All-Purpose Accounts." When applied to long-term transactions they may be known as "Continuous Secured Accounts." They have obvious appeal, but watch your step. It is often difficult to find out just how much you are paying in interest charges. The bank, retailer, or finance company is supposed to tell you (application forms should mention the annual percentage rate) not only to prevent nasty surprises later on, but to enable you to shop around for the best "buy." However, they don't always do so: they rely on the fact that most prospective buyers are more concerned with the amount they are expected to put down, and the monthly repayments, than with interest rates.

RIGGING THE MARKET
An attempt to create an artificial situation in the market for a particular stock. This can be done in a number of ways, but an essential prerequisite is a "thin" market, meaning that there is not a lot of stock in circulation. It's clearly difficult to rig the market in popular stocks like Xerox, IBM, or General Motors, because a significant increase in price could bring out sellers.

But a small family-controlled company, which has marketed only a small proportion of its shares, is in a very different position. The outside speculator may very well succeed in pushing up the price by buying a number of shares and spreading rumors of an impending "favorable development." This is share-pushing, pure and simple. Under stock exchange rules, the people who deal in shares are compelled to deliver stock once they have entered into a firm verbal commitment. The stock may not actually be in their possession, and they usually rely on the probability that a higher price will bring in sellers. (This is what financial journalists mean when they say that the market is "short of stock.") The rigger can afford to play a waiting game. If he has picked the right victim, the response, in terms of price, will be quite out of proportion to the amount of buying. He waits until the price has risen to a totally artificial level and then sells all or part of his holding. The chief losers, as a rule, are less skillful speculators who thought they were on to a good thing but have simply been taken along for the ride. (See also TIPSTER.)

RIGHTS ISSUE
An issue of new shares to existing stockholders, who have the "right" to buy them at a certain price. There may, or may not, be an element of profit in such an issue; in any event, stockholders need not necessarily take up the new shares. It is, however, well to consult one's broker because inaction may mean a loss. Rights issues are a useful way for companies to raise money, especially at times when the market is buoyant. But they are not always popular with investors, and the share price often falls slightly when one is announced.

Companies also issue pieces of paper called "warrants." These are similar to rights, except that they are much more long-lived. They may be good for years, or even forever. (Some are "callable," meaning the issuing company has the right to buy them back at any time it wishes, and most warrants have an expiration date beyond which they are worthless. It pays to check.)

The best-known warrants are sold on the American Stock Exchange, but the majority trade over the counter. Each one represents a right to buy a certain share of stock at a fixed price. This price is invariably well above the current market level, so you don't make any money unless the stock itself shows a very substantial rise.

ROBBER BARONS

A label first used by the embattled farmers of Kansas, in one of their antimonopoly pamphlets of 1880, to describe the masters of the American railway system. It was part of an extraordinary age — the period of America's industrial revolution. The number of manufacturing workers rose from two million in 1869 to ten million in 1929, and total manufacturing output increased nearly twenty-fold. "It was," Professor Prescott wrote in *Financing American Enterprise*, "an age of rough and tumble pursuit of wealth and power."

One of the best-known robber barons was John Pierpont Morgan. Morgan was primarily an investment banker. In other words, he was an expert in the flotation of securities, rather than in the normal banking activity of taking deposits and making loans. He helped to form new corporations, and to provide extra finance for existing ones, by buying newly issued securities from them at wholesale and placing them with investors at retail. He used his own funds to gain options on railroad or industrial capital, and then worked hard to sell this capital to the public at home and abroad. Given the vast and rapidly growing need for finance during this exciting period, this was obviously a field which offered immense scope. Morgan made the most of it. But he was much more than a promoter, a simple manufacturer of stock. He built a great financial empire which controlled large sections of the economy, created monopoly situations, made and unmade other empires, and on one occasion even bailed out the US treasury. His influence was so enormous that Wall Street wags dubbed him "Pierpontifex Maximus."

If his activities meant clashes with the law — well, no matter. One of the many anecdotes told about him has a lawyer saying about some audacious proposal: "I don't think you can legally do that." Morgan replied coldly: "Well, I don't know as I want a lawyer to tell me what I cannot do. I hire him to tell me how to do what I want to do." On the eve of a threatened antitrust suit, Morgan informed President Theodore Roosevelt: "If we have done anything wrong, send your man [the Attorney General] to my man, and they can fix things up."

If Morgan had been born into the present generation, he would have found life much more frustrating; security regulations and antitrust laws introduced partly because of his own skillful operations have made it difficult to build another Morgan empire.

RUNAWAY INFLATION
See HYPERINFLATION.

S

SATELLITE MANAGEMENT
See PROJECT MANAGEMENT.

SATISFACTORY
The most overworked word in a company chairman's vocabulary. It can be used to cover a multitude of possibilities. At one extreme it may mean a 30 per cent rise in profits; the chairman only calls it "satisfactory progress" because he doesn't want any stockholders to think that success is making him complacent. At the other, it may mean a 10 per cent fall in profits. The chairman will simply blame the government, or the weather, or whatever else happens to be handy, and announce that the figures are "satisfactory in the circumstances." Used in forecasts, the word is almost meaningless and ought to be banned. Investors should certainly not allow themselves to be misled by it.

SCARCE CURRENCY CLAUSE
A clause in the articles of the International Monetary Fund which enables member countries to impose discriminatory import restrictions against a country whose currency has been officially declared "scarce." The idea was to have some weapon against governments which deliberately kept their currencies undervalued, so that their exporters would have an extra advantage in world trading markets. The offended parties would complain to the International Monetary Fund, which would then give its official blessing to retaliatory steps. It was thought, of course, that the mere threat would normally be enough to achieve the desired effect. The clause, certainly, has been invoked on very few occasions. When President Nixon took action, in the summer of 1971, to "protect the dollar," he did not single out the Japanese — even though the yen could very easily have been declared a scarce currency. He imposed a general import surcharge on foreign products instead. This, no doubt,

was partly because Washington has disliked the clause ever since the postwar years when the obvious candidate for discrimination was the dollar.

SCARSDALE FATS

Nickname said to have been invented by Boston institutions for a heavyweight Wall Street stockbroker who specializes in brain-picking sessions over lunch. I am not one to give away true identities, but I was once approached by a heavyweight Wall Street stockbroker called Bob Brimberg and asked to attend just such a lunch. He suggested that I should talk to his guests, about the pound or whatever else took my fancy, and added that for this rather pleasant duty (I was then a financial editor, in New York to gather views for my column) I would be paid a fee of $500. In London one is expected to talk for free, so I accepted with alacrity. Halfway through lunch, Mr. Brimberg's *modus operandi* became brilliantly clear. He made a point of inviting investment managers whose business he hoped to get to come and listen, over the scampi and iced water, to a guest who would reveal all. I hardly matched up to his usual standard — my immediate predecessor had been Everett Dirksen — but I gather that my fee matched my status. Mr. Brimberg was solely interested in making contact with people who wouldn't have bothered with him otherwise, and we were the bait. I admired the way he went to work, but I'm bound to say that when, a few months later, he tried the same ploy in London it was not a success. At his request, and for a substantial fee, I invited twenty leading City investment managers to the Savoy for dinner. They had a good time — until Mr. Brimberg made it clear that they were expected to get down to business. English City gentlemen are as eager as anyone else to make money (and often more ruthless than their American rivals) but they like to keep up the pretense that it's a sideline — not to be discussed, in blunt fashion, over brandy and cigars.

SECURITIES AND EXCHANGE COMMISSION
An official watchdog, popularly known as the SEC, which is supposed to regulate the securities industry in the United States. It has considerable powers, and occasionally uses them. Over the years, however, the SEC has pushed Wall Street toward a policy of "self-regulation" — a bureaucratic euphemism, some say, for no regulation whatever. Much the same is true of Britain, which has no official body like the SEC. The Stock Exchange Council, the Bank of England, and other financial bodies usually try to insure that the rules are followed: in obvious cases of abuse, the Board of Trade is empowered to step in. There is also a City Fraud Squad, made up of policemen with accountancy degrees or other financial qualifications, which watches out for currency frauds and other infringements of the law.

SELLERS' MARKET
One in which conditions are favorable to sellers, usually because demand is bigger than supply. If people want more copies of this book than the publisher has printed, and he is unwilling to produce more, he is in a sellers' market. He may raise the price, and generally do his best to exploit the situation. Sellers' markets are caused by many factors. In wartime, rationing and transport difficulties may be the chief reasons. If rapid inflation — too much money chasing too few goods — is added to this, sellers tend to have it all their own way. In peacetime, the manufacturer of an unusual and attractive new product may deliberately restrict

deliveries to retailers, so that he can keep the price high. It's usually not very long before a rival provides some competition, but sometimes a sellers' market may continue for years.

A buyers' market is exactly the opposite: it may arise from overproduction, or a sudden fall in demand, and is usually associated with business recessions.

SELL HALF

Advice given by professional investment advisers who want to keep their clients happy. I once knew a financial editor who made this his set answer to every inquiry. He was highly popular. Every stockbroker and financial journalist knows that advice to sell *everything* is risky. If the stock goes up afterward, you will be bitterly criticized for depriving your customer of an easy profit. If you make your advice public — either through a financial column or through a monthly stockbrokers' circular — people will accuse you of deliberately driving the price down. "Sell half" is the kind of compromise solution that appeals to everyone.

Professionals know, of course, that selling at the right moment is an essential part of successful investment — and even more so of speculation. Amateurs tend to care too much about the price they paid; if they show a loss, they usually hang on in the desperate hope that, sooner or later, the shares will get back to the old level. Sometimes they never do. More often, it takes years to reach the original price. By cutting his loss, and reinvesting in a more promising stock, the holder could have done much better.

The way to speculate successfully is to take a long series of small losses and one great big profit. Sell if you bought a stock for a particular reason, and that reason proves to be wrong. Don't invent other reasons for holding on.

SELLING SHORT
The favorite activity of the bear. Basically it means selling stock you haven't got (but can borrow) in the hope that, by the time you have to deliver, the price will have declined. You buy at the lower level, deliver, and pocket the difference.

Selling short requires skill in timing, courage, and luck. Some people regard it as thoroughly un-American, because it is downbeat and serves no purpose other than to enrich the person doing it. The Securities and Exchange Commission, too, takes a critical view of such speculative activity. Regulations may be essential, if only to prevent excess, but I can't see why short selling should be regarded as un-American: to me it seems the very essence of capitalism. (See also MARGIN BUYING and SPECULATOR.)

SERVICE CONTRACT
An arrangement devised to insure that key executives stay in their jobs. It usually covers a period from one to five years. Good men are not easy to come by, and sensible firms try to make sure that they are not lured away by rivals. Sometimes, of course, things go wrong. An executive may not live up to his early promise, or he may disagree with the rest of the board on how the company should be run. The service contract can, in those circumstances, be terminated on payment of compensation.

Take-over bids and mergers have added an interesting new twist to the game. Directors who have reason to suspect that someone may try to bid for their firm invariably take a quick look at their service contracts. If they have only short periods to run, they vote themselves new five-year agreements. In other words, the bidder may find that, if he succeeds in winning control, it will cost him a very large sum of money to change the board. There are several examples of bids which were withdrawn after the board's stratagem became known; the people who suffered were, of course, the unsuspecting stockholders.

SHOE RIOT
One of the more extravagant phrases used by American retail firms (in this case shoe shops) to attract customers. "Storm" is another favorite. A "clothing storm" is considered to be a much more exciting concept than a mere sale. One advertisement which caught my eye, not along ago, was aimed at the Greenwich Village set. "We've got a surplus hang-up," it announced, "it comes on every time you make the scene at Kaufman — where the in look blows your mind and keeps your bread cool." Wow!

SLUMP
The most dramatic of the three stages in economic downturns — recession, depression, slump. Its outward symptoms are high unemployment and a fall in production, profits, and prices. Newspapers love the word, because it fits easily into a headline and tends to make a big impact. It therefore tends to be used more often than circumstances really justify. Slumps often follow a boom which has got out of hand; the first real sign of downturn sends people into a panic because they are overcommitted, and their reaction tends to have a chain effect. Governments nowadays try to avoid rapid changes from boom to slump by frequent adjustments in key factors such as interest rates and taxation, but experience shows that, once people have convinced themselves that things are bad, it takes a long time to restore confidence. (See BUSINESS CONFIDENCE.)

SOCIAL INFLATION

Phrase used to describe the escalating costs of doing business in an era of rapid social change. Pollution control is an obvious example. Others include increased attention to safety both in products and on the job, exhortations from social activists that industry get more involved in solving community problems, and demands for a shorter workweek, more liberal pensions, and expanded fringe benefits. Many of these costs are being passed on to buyers of goods and services in the form of higher prices. "It's a wonderful thing to have clear air, clean water, better medical care," says one company president. "Nobody can be against these things. But people must realize they are going to have to pay."

Did I hear you suggest that corporations ought to be satisfied with lower profits? You must be joking.

SOUTH SEA BUBBLE

If you think speculators were crazy in 1929, and still have a tendency toward madness today, you should have been around when this one burst.

Early in the eighteenth century a vast number of wild financial projects were launched in Britain. Many of the new companies had bizarre objectives such as "importing a large number of jackasses from Spain" and "fishing wrecks from the Irish coast." One company announced, simply, that it was being formed "for an undertaking which shall in due time be revealed." The promoter disappeared that same day.

The peak of this tomfoolery came when the famous South Sea Company, originally formed to develop South American and Pacific trade, offered to take over the national debt and issued shares for this purpose. The whole country (including the king and Parliament) became involved and the shares rose to ten times their nominal values. Fortunes were made and lost — until the company suddenly collapsed in 1720. The result, inevitably, was financial chaos. More than a hundred years went by before Parliament allowed the formation of companies again, and then only on very strict conditions.

SPECIAL DRAWING RIGHTS

In banking and academic circles, it's smart to call them SDR's. In the newspaper world, they are usually known as "paper gold." Actually, they are neither gold nor paper but, very simply, an allocation of automatic credit lines which can be used between different countries. They serve as extra reserves at a time of balance-of-payments difficulties. They are not meant to be a *substitute* for getting the balance of payments right, nor are they a panacea for the problems of the international monetary system. SDR's are valuable chiefly because they represent a firm departure from man's slavery to gold, for so long the pivot of the system. The SDR scheme is administered by the International Monetary Fund and it took years to get agreement among the hundred-plus countries which belong to this twentieth-century version of a mutual aid society. Monetary puritans still dislike it.

SPECIALIST

A Wall Street broker who confines his activities to a group of stocks sold at one trading post. He never moves away from that spot, so he is always there to accept orders from other brokers, or, for a fee, to take on the broker's order and execute it himself.

The specialist is the key man in every deal, but the specialist system is no careful scientific construction. It just grew that way. It all began one day when a New York Stock Exchange member broke his leg and had to remain stationary. Other brokers began to deposit their orders in certain stocks with him, for a fee, and eventually he found this sufficiently lucrative for him to stay in one place and "specialize" in those stocks. With a thin electronic overlay, that is how the system operates today. Many people think it is no longer appropriate, given the vastly increased trading volume, and steps have been taken toward creating a computerized market. But traditions are not easily broken, and the specialist knows how to look after his interests. He'll be around for quite a while to come. (See also FLOOR BROKER.)

SPECULATOR

Every politician's favorite scapegoat. In the communist world he has long been an officially designated villain. He loyally served Marx, Lenin, and Mao Tse-tung — indeed, it is no exaggeration that, without him, the communist system might never have come into being. He was, and still is, the man everyone loves to hate.

The Soviets have never thanked the speculator, or at least acknowledged their debt to him. Nor, for that matter, have the Chinese. If there is one thing which unites this vast, mysterious country, it is a Peking-inspired-and-approved contempt for speculation. Next to the warlords of the Pentagon, the speculator is the one figure still clearly identifiable as the arch enemy.

What really hurts, however, is that the speculator has, over the years, found himself increasingly condemned by his own side. The London Stock Exchange disowned him a long time ago. Needled by phrases like "gambling casino" and "speculators' paradise," the gentlemen who run this august institution insisted that they had never really approved of him. The stock exchange, we were told, existed to serve *investors* — worthy citizens prepared to back Britain by putting their life savings into solid blue chips. It did not, repeat not, exist to make money for idle, unscrupulous rascals who had no interest beyond buying and selling. I have never quite understood why the stock exchange should be so anxious to reject the profit motive. Backing Britain is all very well, but making a few thousand overnight is even better. Any member of the stock exchange who says otherwise is a hypocrite — or an idealist who should seek a different profession.

It was easier to accept the Macmillan government's decision to punish speculators by introducing a new tax on capital gains. The chancellor of the day was trying to get the unions' cooperation on wages and, like all those who followed him, he thought it could be won attacking their traditional enemy. It didn't work. The tax, however, stayed. So did ministerial dislike of the speculator. Harold Wilson used to get terribly angry about the "maneuvering of odious speculators"; the successive "waves of speculation"; the "speculation at home and abroad." In speech after speech he conjured up visions of a sinister, tightly knit group of politically motivated men hell-bent on "selling Britain short." The speculator, it appeared, spent his day swigging brandy and communicating absurd gossip to Paris and Zürich. His sole interest was in bringing Labour — and, therefore, the country — to its ruin. When sterling was devalued in 1967, Harold naturally blamed the speculators. And guess who lost him the 1970 general election? Right first time.

In 1971, President Nixon joined the game. Richard Nixon! Hero of the Republican party, titular head of the capitalist world. Generations of Americans have been brought up to believe in the virtues of making a fast buck. Every library has dozens of books on the subject. America might have much to apologize for — but speculation? Surely not. Yet here was Mr. Nixon, condemning the poor speculator for "waging all-out war against the dollar" and "thriving on crises."

Who are the speculators? In the currency field, mostly bankers paid to make the best use of their clients' money, or the finance directors of big corporations which have entered into extensive commitments abroad. They don't like the word "speculation"; in their book, it is called "money management." Businessmen, they say, do not have a patriotic duty to risk losses or forgo a possible profit: it's the job of governments to maintain confidence in currency. (See BEAR.)

SPIT

An organization existing solely in the mind of the author, but essential if we want to avoid chaos. SPIT is short for "Society to Prevent the Initials Trend," and is dedicated to preserving Shakespeare's language from the relentless attacks of economists, businessmen, and bureaucrats. The human race, it seems, has an insatiable urge to set up more and more committees and organizations. And each one insists, sooner or later, on being known by its initials. We have UNO, UNESCO, NATO, SEATO, WHO, GATT, and NIBMAR, and we have innumerable trade organizations which feel deeply insulted if you don't immediately appreciate the significance of letters like BEMA and SIMA.

The same applies if you visit the United States or Germany. The merger mania in industry ought to have cut down the number of initials, but the opposite is true. Faced with the need to find a new title which describes their extended range of activities, company boards invariably fall back on initials. Occasionally, some brave fellow makes a plea for originality but is usually slapped down on the grounds that it would be tragic to lose the good will attached to a name built up over the years. Initials tend to be regarded as the next best thing. Ultimately, we may have to start talking in this crazy language, for fear of not being with it. "Good morning, EBD. RST here. Have you seen that letter from UDT? They want to know if we have talked to BSA and WGI. They think IBI may be worth contacting too." SOS!

STAG
British term for what is, next to bulls and bears, the most ferocious of stock exchange animals. Well, he's not all that ferocious, really. It would be fascinating to know why the early, brandy-swigging stockbrokers were so desperately anxious to pick these virility symbols; why not pigs, ducks, and geese?

A stag is one who subscribes to new issues on the market, not with the noble aim of holding them as an investment, but with the base desire to name a quick killing (Aha! There's your answer). He looks out for companies whose shares are coming onto the market for the first time, and if they seem likely to appeal to investors he fills in an application form. Or, more probably, several application forms. Such forms are published in one or more newspapers and hardened stags have been known to fill in up to a hundred of them using all types of names. Some are always genuine: it's marvelous how many aunts you can find when money is involved. Others are pure invention. The stock exchange, alas, has clamped down on this kind of activity and the stag's life is nowadays much more difficult. The world, sad to say, is full of spoilsports.

STAGFLATION

A hybrid meaning that the economy is making no headway — stagnating — and having inflation at the same time. It's really the worst of both worlds and difficult to cure.

STATISTICS

Tabulated numerical facts. We trust them more than we trust politicians. People lie, but figures tell the truth. Or so it's said. The reality is different. Statistics can be made to dance to any tune you want to play. You can put favorable factors in, and leave others out. You can adjust, revise, ignore. And you can twist the end product. Successive election campaigns have shown how eminently twistable statistics can be. No one is lying; he is interpreting figures in a way favorable to his own argument. To one party, a large balance-of-payments deficit is the most frightful catastrophe. To another, it is a minor problem.

In 1969, the Polish Embassy in London — of all things — discovered that Britain's Board of Trade, with its computers and highly trained officials, had somehow managed to mislay $27 million a month for the past six years. It meant that, throughout the long and costly financial crisis, we had consistently underrated our strength. Indeed, one treasury official was quoted as saying that devaluation would have been unnecessary if the error had been discovered sooner. The people who compile statistics know, of course, how unreliable they can be. This is why officials always make a point of drawing attention to the small print. Civil servants have little time for ministers and impatient industrialists who want "one figure, with no ifs and buts." At best, figures are no more than a guide. At worst, they point away from the truth.

Statistics, alas, have increasingly become a substitute for argument, and a good memory for facts and figures is generally regarded as superior to a thoughtful mind. People have come to accept this to such an extent that you can get away with making up figures on the spot, as long as you sound confident enough in your delivery. Try it next time you get into a boring argument at a dinner party. Do me one favor, though. When you have won your case, confess what you have been doing. Your fellow men won't thank you for exposing their gullibility, but you will have done them a service.

39 ¼ 23 DAVIS 1.50 122 35 36 ½ 33 36 + 1.
Not, as you may think, a series of totally meaningless figures (even though I have made them up) but the way newspapers like the *Wall Street Journal* list stocks. The dollar sign is invariably dropped for brevity. Prices are quoted in dollars and fractions, rather than dollars and cents, so 25 cents is shown as ¼. It's also worth remembering that brokers count changes in "points": a dollar increase in price means the stock is "up a point."

The first two figures are the highest and lowest prices at which the stock has sold during the year. I have always found this very useful, partly because it indicates the kind of fluctuation one can expect, and partly because it shows how near the top — or bottom — I am buying at a given moment. The fact that a stock is at, or close to, the year's high often deters people in search of bargains. But, of course, it does not automatically mean that the price cannot go higher. It generally indicates that the company is doing well, or that a situation is developing which makes *some* investors think the stock is worth backing. By the same token, a stock is not necessarily cheap because it happens to be at the year's low. There are usually very good reasons why this should be so, and it certainly pays to investigate before you leap.

The highs and lows are followed by the company name, and after that comes the dividend paid on the stock for the past year — in this case, $1.50 a share. Note the word "past": there is no guarantee, with a common stock, that you will get exactly the same next time. Companies try to maintain at least a steady dividend record, because it is important for their market rating, but like everyone else they do have their ups and downs. Sometimes you will notice symbols right after the dividend; the explanations for these are offered at the end of the stock listings and are well worth looking at, if only because they may contain a warning.

The number following the dividend figure represents the day's trading volume in hundreds of shares. In other words, 12,200 shares in Davis, Inc., were bought and sold during the day. Volume is important because it indicates the level of interest in the stock, but it obviously makes sense to watch it over a period of time rather than a single day. A sudden, sharp upturn may not be very significant, but if sustained over, say, a week it may well indicate some important development.

Whether the development is expected to be good or bad should be apparent from the next set of figures. They describe the day's price movements — opening price, high price for the day, low price, and closing price. The final figure shows the net change of the day; in this case, the stock was selling at a price $1 higher than at the end of trading on the previous day.

Stock market listings are, obviously, a handy guide to what is going on. But they do not, of course, tell the whole story and it's risky to jump to conclusions.

STOCK OPTIONS

A means of giving senior employees a share in the prosperity of a company. The basic idea is simple: it's easier to attract the right managerial talent, and to keep it keen, if one can offer more than the usual salary and perks. So you give your key people an option to take up stock, requiring from them only a nominal sum for the privilege. If they rise in value, they are free to sell and make a profit. Necessary incentive or big business fiddle? The truth, as economists like to say, probably lies somewhere in between. It is a "fiddle" of sorts. On the other hand there's much to be said for giving the new breed of managers a chance to build up the kind of capital needed to insure financial independence. The need to play safe can, and does, stifle enterprise and gives too much power to the institutions which control the purse strings.

STOCK SPLIT

An issue of new stock to stockholders without their having to put up any further money. You end up with more paper, but your holding may not be worth any more because the market automatically adjusts the price to allow for the issue. The same happens with dividends. Stock splits are nevertheless popular because they do tend to have a beneficial effect. New investors, for example, are often put off by a "heavy" price — say $50 a share — and buy much more readily if it is split. This, of course, helps the existing holders. Corporations, moreover, often try to give investors at least a modest effective increase in dividend.

STOP-GO
A familiar feature of the British postwar financial and economic scene. It means, very simply, sharp changes in direction at uncomfortably frequent intervals. The pattern goes something like this. The economy is sluggish, unemployment is high, and the Government is urged to do something about it. It cuts taxes, makes credit easier, lowers interest rates, and generally sets the lights to "go." A few months later, though, it appears that this bold strategy is damaging the balance of payments. We import too much, pay ourselves too much in wages, and generally live beyond our long-term means. The pound comes under pressure, and we are right in the middle of another financial crisis. To counter it, the Government raises taxes, makes credit harder to get, boosts interest rates, and generally sets the lights to "stop."

Stop-go has happened so often that businessmen have become highly skeptical about government forecasts. We need a period of sustained advance, say five years, before most of them will really believe that we have managed to get away from it.

STUDY IN DEPTH
Anything that takes time. Governments like to use it to postpone decisions which may, for the moment, be too costly or politically awkward. By ordering a study in depth, and announcing the fact to the public, they can convey the impression that something is being done. Politicians usually know perfectly well that the study will achieve nothing, and that it will join earlier studies on some bureaucratic shelf, unloved and forgotten. But that's not the point: if it keeps critics quiet, the study has achieved its purpose. A recur-

ring example is a study in depth of the endemic unemployment problem of Britain's regions. The Government has commissioned endless studies on the subject, and is fully aware that nothing short of growth in the economy as a whole will ever provide a satisfactory answer. And yet, each time unemployment rises to embarrassing levels, it reacts by ordering yet another study in depth. We are asked not to be cynical about our politicians, and perhaps it's unfair that we should be. They are, after all, to a very considerable extent at the mercy of events. But it becomes increasingly difficult to go along with this particular charade.

SUBSIDIARY

Also known as "offshoot." A company in which another holds more than half of the voting shares. This gives it the right to appoint directors and direct boardroom decisions. Many subsidiaries are "wholly owned"; Ford of Britain, for example, is a wholly owned subsidiary of Ford US. But there are also companies in which the public has minority stake. The minority stockholder has certain rights, but he is to a large extent at the mercy of the "parent company" or "holding company" which exercises control. Dividends, for example, may be deliberately kept down. On the other hand, he sometimes benefits from a major expansion program made possible by the parent's vast resources, or from the injection of technological expertise. It is always possible, too, that the parent will one day decide to make an offer for the minority holdings — in which case there could be a useful capital gain.

SUBSIDY

A government grant of money to a company, local authority, or industry. Most governments nowadays make considerable use of subsidies. They may, for example, decide that the public interest demands low prices for farm products and pay farmers the difference between a mutually agreed level and what they are able to get in the open market. Or they may use state money to finance public housing projects and charge low-income tenants a rent which any normal landlord would regard as uneconomic. Aid to regions, to make up for lack of raw materials or some other weakness, has also grown more common. And, of course, governments frequently subsidize public services such as transport, and special projects which are thought worthwhile from a national point of view — such as space travel — but which are not viable on strictly commercial considerations. Theaters, art galleries, museums, and many other useful features of modern civilized life all benefit from government subsidies.

In theory, there is no limit to the game. There is certainly no shortage of worthy causes, and of demands for help. In practice, though, governments have to draw the line somewhere if they want to stay in power. Subsidies are part of government expenditure, and high expenditure can only be sustained, in the long run, by high taxation.

SURVIVAL

The art, usually complex, of remaining a Higher Executive. Memorize the following eight basic rules, and you'll be all right:

(1) Don't become a big businessman

This is an elementary precaution, but it's remarkable how many intelligent people ignore it. Experience shows that life is much safer just below the top. In Washington top officials wield more power, earn more money, and stay around longer than their alleged, overpublicized political masters. In industry the men who have charge of the purse — usually accountants — have developed an enviable resistance to purges. It's the chief executive, the man who makes decisions which involve a large element of risk, whose head is sacrificed when things go wrong. And yet the man below the top probably has much the same after-tax income as his vulnerable chairman. Choose your place, well away from the founder's portrait, and refuse to budge. Resist all offers of promotion — and arrange to be out of town whenever important decisions are being taken.

(2) Remember, Khrushchev danced the Gopak
. . . and if he'd carried on dancing, he would still be one of Russia's leaders today. Violent exercise of this kind may not suit you, but there are plenty of equivalents. It is, for example, useful to be able to play a third-rate game of golf. Any fool can play well; it takes real skill to play just that little bit worse than the man you are trying to impress. Beating him is the surest way to get pushed out, and losing unconvincingly will make him doubt your integrity. The trick is to let him win by a slender margin: it will make you an indispensable partner.

(3) Cultivate Wall Street
Because that's where the power lies. Wall Street institutions are the biggest stockholders in industry, and they have become significantly militant. When a company runs into trouble, it's Wall Street which forces changes in management. Let a banker or investment manager win on the golf course, and you're secure for life.

(4) Don't talk, listen
It's easy to talk yourself into trouble. You may, for example, object to some proposal on the grounds that it is both absurd and illogical. This, as any skilled survivor will tell you, is naive. Your fellow executives will never forgive you. Sooner or later you will be tempted to present your own proposal. It will be accepted with alacrity — and, three months later, you will be held to account for the consequences. Be noncommittal. Listen. People love good listeners: they tend to be praised as great conversationalists.

(5) Don't say no

Superiors are often heard to say that they don't want yes men. This is a lie: they do. If the top man wants to win an argument, let him. But it's good strategy, just occasionally, to make him wait a few seconds for your yes. Darryl Zanuck once snapped at an overeager assistant: "Don't say yes until I've finished talking."

(6) Beware of politicians

People in power move around so fast that it doesn't pay to get friendly. If you are known to be on good terms with one, the next one will almost certainly want to make an example out of you — just to show that he disagrees with his predecessor. If a secretary of state enters a room, try to make an excuse and leave. Refuse to be drawn into making an open statement of support for any party: if, by some mischance, you are forced to make a speech stick to platitudes used and accepted by both sides. You're on safe ground if you point out that "the world does not owe us a living," and refer to "the golden thread running through our history." It's also safe to suggest that we must "wage war on inefficiency" and "meet the challenge of the seventies."

(7) Never resign

"Only fools resign," Lord Beaverbrook once told me — and, of course, he was right. Most people offer their resignation in the certainty that it won't be accepted. They consider themselves indispensable, and are surprised to find that others don't agree. By then it's usually too late. If you are angry, beat your wife or kick the dog. Don't let anyone goad you into resigning: remember that people who leave voluntarily rarely collect compensation. If you want to leave, goad them into sacking you. If you want to stay, ignore their hints. It's surprising how many executives threatened with dismissal have kept their jobs by pretending to be deaf.

(8) Ignore failures

They may be nice fellows — indeed, they almost invariably are — but it's unwise to associate with losers. You've heard of guilt by association? Well then.

T

TAKE A BATH
Something no stock market operator ever wants to do. It means losing a lot of money. Taking a bath is like "going to the cleaners" or "falling out of bed" — a nasty reminder that playing the market is not as simple as it looks.

The dream of every speculator is to "make a killing." I have no idea how speculative gains first became associated with death, but the phrase certainly sounds more dramatic than "making a living." To kill you must become either a bull or a bear, and it's a good idea to avoid cats and dogs. They're speculative stocks of doubtful merit and quite likely to send you straight to the cleaners.

TAKE-OVER BID
An attempt by one company to buy control of another. Because the phrase implies aggression, most bidders prefer to use the more conciliatory word "merger." The end result, though, tends to be much the same.

Bids and mergers fall into three main categories, depending largely on the company making the offer. First, and historically most logical, there is the offer made by a company for another doing the same kind of work. This is known as a "horizontal" merger. If, for example, two companies manufacturing lawn mowers decided to get together, it would be a horizontal merger. It may arise from several motives. The bidder may want to reduce competition and increase his share of the market. He may want to acquire added plant and equipment similar to his own, in order to take advantage of growing demand for his products. Or he may simply want to achieve the economies to be had from pooling resources. Costs per unit tend to decline as the scale of production increases, and mergers can be a quick way of securing cost reductions.

The second type of merger is known as "vertical." It covers the linking of firms at immediately related stages of production and distribution. The buyer may merge with or acquire a company on which he either relies for his supplies, or to which he sells much of his output. The one deal will insure that raw materials and components essential to his basic business will always be available, at a price over which he has control. The other will put him closer to the consumer. It may, for example, enable him to cut out the wholesaler and deal directly with the retail trade.

The third type of merger is the conglomerate, and this involves the merger or acquisition of a company whose activities are in an entirely different sphere.

Take-over bids and mergers are as old as business itself. There have been several merger waves, on both sides of the Atlantic, during the past one hundred years. Many of industry's big names are composite creations. But, as I showed in my book *Merger Mania*, the outcome is often disappointing. The economies of scale tend to take longer to achieve than the bidder would have investors believe at the time of the deal — and size can produce all kinds of problems. The largest company is not necessarily the most efficient or even the most profitable. If size is the prime objective the company can topple under its own weight.

Many companies, too, merge for reasons which have little or nothing to do with industrial logic. Big companies often buy up others solely to prevent a rival from getting them first. This may produce a merger which is structurally all wrong. The same goes for purely defensive marriages, arranged to avoid the embraces of an unwanted partner. It's astonishing how many deals are based on hunches rather than careful calculation; the age of allegedly sophisticated management still has a large number of top executives flying by the seat of their pants.

TASK-FORCE MANAGEMENT
See PROJECT MANAGEMENT.

TAX AVOIDANCE
The lawful part of what is more popularly known as "tax dodging." The law makes a clear distinction between evasion and avoidance. Evasion is deliberate fraud — you know you ought to declare, say, a capital gain on a stock market operation, but do not do so. Avoidance is to know the nature of the tax, and the ways of skating around it through full use of allowances and one or another of the many complex financial schemes — all strictly legal — thought up by clever tax accountants.

Even so, an awful lot of nonsense is talked about allegedly despicable behavior of people who choose to arrange their affairs in such a way as to suit themselves rather than the tax man. Film stars who choose to make their home Switzerland, rather than the country of their birth, are frequently accused of being unpatriotic. And there is, invariably, much criticism of wealthy people who find perfectly legitimate ways of minimizing estate duty.

In France, during 1972, a "tax scandal" blew up around the prime minister, M. Chaban-Delmas. The Paris satirical weekly *Le Canard Enchaîné* alleged that he had managed to escape all taxation from 1966 to 1970. The finance minister, M. Giscard D'Estaing, went on national television to explain how this sort of thing was possible under the French system of tax credits, and pointed out that everyone else could do the same. In other words, if the affair struck people as unjust, it was the system which deserved the blame, not the individual. There is, arguably, something wrong with a tax structure which allows highly placed — and wealthy — people to get away with not paying any taxes. Perhaps the affair will lead to changes. M. Chaban-Delmas was, however, well within his lawful rights, and not even his fiercest critics dared claim that the government had rigged the system with an eye to purely personal gain. No one owes a duty to pay more than the law demands; it's only evasion of the law which can cause you trouble.

TAX HAVEN
Any place which helps foreigners to avoid paying taxes, or at least to keep a substantially bigger part of their income than they would be allowed to at home. Switzerland is perhaps the best-known example; its unique combination of political stability, banking secrecy, highly developed financial expertise, and low rate of tax have attracted many famous residents. Foreigners living in Switzerland but not gainfully employed there are taxed solely on an amount equivalent to five times the rental value of their property. The tiny principality of Liechtenstein is another well-known tax haven, but it does not encourage new residents:

its main appeal is to corporations. One popular corporate device is the foreign-based "holding company." A foreign firm may transfer money earned outside its own country to, say, a holding company in Liechtenstein. Such a company has to have a local director, but there is no reason why it should not be wholly owned by the foreign firm. The money thus transferred by the owner will usually avoid most, if not all taxation. The Bahamas also offer a wide range of services and are more pleasant to live in than other tax havens. There is no income tax, no capital gains tax, and no estate duty. But if you haven't yet made your first million, there is one drawback: the high cost of living. This, indeed, tends to be a problem with most tax havens (it certainly applies to Switzerland) and can be a nuisance. There's not much point, after all, in cutting your tax bill if all the other bills soar.

Nearer home, the Channel Islands and the Isle of Man both rate as tax havens because they have no capital gains tax or estate duty, and income tax is substantially less than in areas which are under the direct jurisdiction of the Inland Revenue and the treasury. In the Channel Islands income tax has been pegged at twenty pence on the pound since 1940; in the Isle of Man, the rate is twenty-one pence.

TAX-LOSS SELLING

Losses made on an investment can be set off against capital gains tax. If you sell stocks or property on which you show a loss, so that you can establish a claim for relief on profits made elsewhere, the process is known as tax-loss selling. Everyone makes investment mistakes but the tax loss takes some of the sting out of it by letting you profit a little bit more on other successful investments.

TAX REFORMS

A device used by politicians to help with elections. Having so many taxes around has not only enabled governments to keep spending what they like, but has also made it easy for politicians to pose as our saviors. Governments get elected because they promise to deliver us from taxes introduced by other governments. And they win our gratitude by announcing "far-reaching reforms of the whole tax system."

Most of us accept without protest that taxes are a necessary evil. We think ourselves lucky if the administration manages to "give us a little more" — a phrase invented by politicians to disguise the fact that, in reality, they are simply allowing us to *keep* a little more of what we earn. But we do not dispute the government's right to levy taxes, to dispose of the revenue in ways which may run counter to our individual wishes, and to make all kinds of moral judgments in doing so. Nor do we challenge its right to pry into our personal affairs, and to haul us up in court to answer whatever charge the Internal Revenue decides to make against us. We not only agree that the government can do all this, but share its indignation that some people should try to skip through the net by moving to Switzerland or the Bahamas. In short, successive governments have brainwashed us into accepting that the tax burden as a whole is not only inevitable, but also morally correct. It was not always so. Earlier generations put up a long and splendid struggle against taxation. If they had not done so, America might never have won its independence.

The history of taxation is full of cunning tricks played on a gullible electorate. A favorite dodge, for example, has been to use national emergencies as a pretext for introducing temporary taxes which, somehow, turn out to be permanent. This is how Britain first got an income tax in 1799.

The prime minister of the day promised it would be "temporary." Temporary my foot!

TAX SHELTER

Term used in the United States to describe investments which people in the upper tax brackets can use to reduce their tax liabilities. Most tax shelters are set up as limited partnerships so that in the event of losses an investor cannot lose more than he invests. Some shelters, as in oil, farms, groves, vineyards, and real estate, are designed to reduce taxes. Others, because they do not pay off for several years, are designed to put off taxes into the future. Unfortunately, many of these ventures have helped their organizers more than their investors. Middle-income people by the thousands have been deluded into chasing elusive profits, largely in oil and gas deals. Hundreds of wealthy doctors, lawyers, and businessmen have been taken into deals for which they were either unsuited or where enormous sums disappeared through clever bookkeeping. Tax shelters are of doubtful value if the basic economics of a venture are unsound.

TECHNOLOGICAL GAP

First discovered by the Italians, who dubbed it *il gap tecnologico* and later advanced as one of the chief reasons why Britain should be in the Common Market. The gap is between European and American techniques of management and technology. An OECD report in 1967 showed that the United States spends six times as much on research and development as the Common Market and three times as much as Western Europe. Besides spending more, it was also getting better value for the money spent, which was devoted to well-defined ends, whereas the European countries tended to be spread too thinly over many unrelated areas and even lost altogether in abandoned projects like the TSR-2 in Britain and sundry joint enterprises which became too expensive. One result of the technological gap, the report noted, was a rapid increase in American control of the most advanced and fastest-growing branches of European industry. Soon after the report was published, the EEC's Council of Ministers agreed that the Six's scientific and technological research in certain fields should be coordinated, and Mr. Wilson — then prime minister — made a speech in which he offered the Community a seven-point technology plan as a basis for joint action. The Wilson plan was never followed up, and European cooperation still leaves much to be desired. Indeed, the gap still seems to be widening.

THUNDERING HERD
A nickname applied to Merrill Lynch, Pierce, Fenner & Smith, the largest firm of stockbrokers in the world. It seems appropriate.

TIMES-SOTHEBY INDEX
An index, produced in London, which tries to measure the market value of works of art. Art, of course, is one of the more traditional forms of investment. The art galleries and museums maintain that they pay vast sums of money for paintings because they like art. There are also one or two eccentric private collectors who share their view. But this is the kind of sentimental, old-fashioned approach which the financial world rightly deplores.

There are many sound reasons for spending a king's ransom on a bit of old canvas, and art has nothing to do with any of them. It is merely the label which art investment trusts put on their stock in trade. The main reason for buying an expensive painting is that it will go up in price. It is, or should be, a hedge against inflation. Possession of one or two fashionable paintings is also good for business. It not only confirms that the owner is wealthy, but also proves that he has shrewd judgment. A man who can pick paintings which appreciate in value is clearly the kind of chap one ought to back. The wealthy owner of a masterpiece, moreover, can insist that no one reproduces it, for chocolate boxes or cigarette cards, without mentioning his name. This can add up to thousands of dollars' worth of free publicity. Banks are enthusiastic buyers of paintings, because they help to project the right image. If a bank wants to stress that it is well established and solid, it buys an old master. If it wants to demonstrate that it is swinging and with it, it buys ultramodern.

Modern paintings have been fashionable in recent years because banks are wooing young people. An additional factor is that you tend to get more for your money: modern artists are generous with canvas. The Chase Manhattan Bank, like others, has a special art committee which buys paintings for its rapidly expanding international network of branches. There's even an art committee at the International Monetary Fund. The lesson for painters is clear: be modern, stock up with large frames, and keep in mind, at all times, your painting's value as an investment.

TIPSTER
Impolite, but accurate, word for someone who makes his living by telling others what to buy. A popular figure at cocktail parties and afternoon teas. Stock market tipsters tend to be the elite, because the stock exchange has a cachet that race tracks and betting shops can't match, but they are not

necessarily more scientific than other tipsters. They listen to rumors, back hunches, study balance sheets (which are usually out of date by the time they're published), and cultivate contacts in industry and the financial world. Some are unscrupulous: they buy a certain stock, plug it, and get out at a profit as soon as the price goes up. Financial editors seldom do this because they know how easily they could be found out. I know of only one case where an editor played the market in this way. Market professionals noticed that each time a certain stock was tipped, the same broker appeared just beforehand with a buying order and reappeared again just afterward to sell. Inquiries were made, the identity of his client was discovered, a complaint was lodged with the Stock Exchange Council, the council informed the man's boss, and the boss sacked him on the spot.

Successful stock tipping is not as easy as people make out. There is a considerable element of hit-and-miss about it, and even experts frequently get caught. On Wall Street some professionals put their trust in astrology and I once met a banker who solemnly declared that the stock market closely followed the rise and fall in hemlines. (His general rule was: "Don't sell until you see the whites of their thighs." Honestly.) In Britain computers are being used to weigh up the "form" of stocks, but you'd be amazed how many people still rely on a pin. There are, of course, various ways of giving one's tip a good start. The most obvious is to pick a stock in which there is a thin market. Newcomers offer a fairly wide range of choice. A small, promising firm may want a stock quotation. It puts the minimum percentage asked for by the stock exchange on the market. Because it is a go-ahead concern, the newcomer's shares are snapped up by investors and held on a long-term basis. This means that, at any given time, the supply of stock is limited. If the company produces excellent results, or a stock tipster repeatedly draws attention to the high quality of the management, a number of other people may be tempted to have a go. Even a small amount of buying can, in these circumstances, produce quite a sharp rise.

Much the best way of establishing one's reputation as a tipster is to use what I call the "grapeshot" method. You tip thirty stocks at the start of the year, on the principle that there's safety in numbers. They can't *all* go wrong. For good measure, you continue to produce a steady stream of tips during the months that follow. At the end of the year, you simply mention the few which have done well. The other few hundred stocks can be conveniently forgotten; no one wants to hear about failures.

Timing is essential to successful stock tipping, as to so much else. I have, over the years, developed the basic rule: when everyone praises a stock for weeks, and the price moves up sharply, I become extremely cautious. After a lengthy period of popularity, a great many people are waiting to cash in their profit. They continue to talk enthusiastically about the shares, in the hope that others will come in and drive the price higher still, but they are eager to be out at the right moment. The founder of the Rothschild family once said he had made his fortune by always selling too soon: an awful lot of speculators try to do the same. (See also LONG-TERM and SPECULATOR.)

TOMBSTONE

Wall Street's word for the advertisement that shows which investment banks are participating in what new issue. It is a social register that tells a story of patronage, temporary promotion, and perhaps even the odd snub, all superimposed on the pecking order of New York's underwriting and brokerage houses.

"Underwriting," means agreeing — in return for a commission — to take up a certain proportion of new stock issued by a manufacturer or other business enterprise, if that stock has not been bought by the public. In America the underwriting business is somewhat different from what it is in Britain, and more lucrative, because its essence lies in the sale of securities, rather than in shouldering the risks of underpinning them with cash. The gross payment to an underwriting syndicate ranges from 1 per cent for a straight debt to 6 per cent for a common-stock offering.

The Wall Street underwriting club is laid out for all to see on the tombstone of any important issue. It consists of more than twenty houses which among them account for 95 per cent of the value of new issues floated by the private sector in the United States. These are the so-called major houses, and their standing relative to one another depends mainly on the number and importance of their business clients. The tombstones are headed by the names of the managers and list the major participants in alphabetical order; just occasionally, the club may tag on the name of a smaller house that might have talked its way into a major position on the issue.

TRADE CYCLE
See BUSINESS CYCLE.

TRADE GAP
The gap between a country's imports and exports. It's often confused with the balance of payments, and many people wrongly assume it to be the equivalent of a nation's balance sheet. In fact, it is only one of the sheet's items — though, admittedly, often the most important one. Nations like the

United States and Britain, for example, have always had a large income from investments abroad, and from service trades like banking, insurance, and shipping. Britain had a trade gap throughout the second half of the nineteenth century, generally regarded as the peak period of her prosperity. It only became a problem when, in later years, overseas investment declined and governments spent more abroad than the country could really afford. (See also BALANCE OF PAYMENTS, DEVALUATION, and INVISIBLES.)

TREASURY BILL

A piece of paper issued by the United States Treasury which is considered as good as cash — except that you get interest on it. The treasury sells the bills as and when it needs the money: the treasury bill is essentially a short-term debt instrument. Bills can be bought by mail (all that's needed is a certified personal check, made out to the nearest Federal Reserve Bank) and there is no risk whatever. Prospective buyers have a choice of four maturities: three months, six months, nine months, and twelve months. Corporations and financial institutions like them because they're an easy way of earning interest without tying up one's funds. Individual buyers tend to prefer the three-month bills — that is, bills repayable in ninety days. Because bookkeeping costs were getting out of hand, the treasury announced in 1970 that its lowest-denomination bill would be raised from $1000 to $10,000, a decision which was greeted with a storm of protest. Treasury bills are *not* a medium for either savings or investment: they are a temporary shelter. Interest rates depend on money-market conditions, so the treasury bills' appeal is generally greatest when short-term rates are high. At other times you may do just as well, if not better, with an ordinary savings account. (See also MATURITY.)

TREATY OF ROME
Strictly speaking, not one treaty but two. Signed by six countries (Belgium, France, Germany, Italy, Luxembourg, and the Netherlands) in March 1957, they created two communities: a European Economic Community (EEC) to bring into being a single market for all goods and develop a common economic policy; and a European Atomic Energy Community (Euratom) to further the use of nuclear energy in Europe for peaceful purposes. Headquarters were set up in Brussels.

The EEC soon became popularly known as the Common Market. It is an apt description; because of the many objectives laid down in the Treaty of Rome, the creation of a single market, unhampered by customs duties, has actually come about. Economic unity has been much harder to achieve. There is still no European company law, no common currency, no freedom from exchange control. With one or two exceptions, such as the agricultural system, economic and financial policies continue to be made at the national level. Political union seems even further away: there is a European parliament, but no one pays much attention to it. In short, the "Europe" visualized by idealists when the Treaty of Rome was signed does not exist. Surveys suggest that almost all businessmen in the market countries believe that the existence of the EEC has helped them, and Mr. Heath's government insists that it will help Britain, too. This may be so. But we won't see a "United States of Europe," as originally envisaged, in the seventies, and may not even see it by the end of the century.

TRUST-BUSTING
The policy, dating back to the Sherman Anti-Trust Act of 1890, of breaking up monopolies formed by mergers into

their constituent units. For example, in 1911 the Supreme Court ordered the dissolution of the Standard Oil Company of New Jersey, which had acquired the stock of more than seventy oil companies in order to monopolize the trade. The Clayton and Federal Trade Commission Act of 1914 strengthened the hand of the trust-busters, and today antitrust legislation is stronger than in many other countries. Critics, however, not only object to it on ideological grounds, but argue that it has failed to deal with basic monopoly problems. The ideological case rests on the traditional belief in free market forces, but also reflects a deep-rooted respect for, and admiration of, bigness. (The admiration, ironically enough, does not seem to extend to labor unions: many businessmen think they have abused the monopoly powers they were given in the thirties to meet big industry on equal terms, and would dearly love to see them broken up.)

More practical, and for some more persuasive, is the argument that trust-busting has not prevented huge combines from dominating business activity. It certainly has not succeeded in bringing prices and costs under control. The only answer, I suppose, is to ask what would have happened if there had been no antitrust legislation at all. Could free market forces really have been relied upon to serve the best interests of the nation? (See also FREE ENTERPRISE.)

TURNOVER
The value, or volume, of total sales in any one year. Don't make the mistake of confusing it with profit. Some companies publish very impressive turnover figures, and innocent investors have been known to jump to the wrong conclusion. A high turnover isn't much good if you don't make any money on it.

The rate at which goods are sold, or turned over, is clearly much faster in some areas than in others. Food retailing, for example, tends to see rapid turnover at small profit margins. The furniture department of a big store, on the other hand, operates at a much more leisurely pace. It means considerable capital is locked up in stock — but, against this, profit margins tend to be substantially higher. Turnover figures help to show how a company is doing, but they are only a part of the overall picture and therefore need to be approached with caution.

TWO-DOLLAR BROKER
See FLOOR BROKER.

U

UNDERVALUED CURRENCY
One whose official exchange rate (see FIXED PARITY) is maintained below the level it would reach in a free market. The German mark was in that position for a long time. Undervaluation may arise because a country is particularly successful in export markets, or because it is better than others at controlling inflation. It often becomes a source of national pride. The Germans, for example, saw their "strong

mark" as some kind of virility symbol, compensating for all the bruises dealt to their egos by the Second World War. On a more practical level, it kept their exports relatively cheap and so helped to widen their markets. Nor was there any sort of restriction on what people did with their capital abroad: unlike the British, they were free to buy up foreign companies and property without having the treasury look disapprovingly over their shoulders.

Not surprisingly, trade competitors tend to regard deliberate undervaluation as a selfish act. Countries which indulge in it are constantly being urged to fix a new, higher price for their paper money. Sometimes they give way (the Germans have done so) but changes tend to be so small that they do not really make a significant difference for any length of time. The practice of floating currencies has made the general situation much more flexible than before, but the basic point remains the same: an undervalued currency is a sign of success.

UPTICK

Going up; an upward trend. Used both in the stock market and in economic argument. Newspapers often refer to an uptick economy, and I suppose it's as good a word as any.

Stock market analysts also like to refer to a particular stock's "upside potential," meaning the scope for capital gain. "Downside potential" is, you will not be surprised to hear, exactly the opposite. It's all part of the money world's relentless campaign to dazzle outsiders with expertise. It does not, alas, guarantee accuracy.

USURY

Lending money at an exorbitant rate of interest. Shakespeare had a lot to say about it, and it was fiercely condemned by moralists and churchmen of the Middle Ages. The lender was outside the law, expert at deception, and harsh in his treatment of debtors.

The word is rarely used today, not only because lending has become respectable but also because borrowers have all kinds of legal protection and are, in any case, reckoned to be more sophisticated. It isn't always so: starry-eyed young couples who buy, say, a new car on credit are sometimes as much casualties of usury as earlier generations who got taken for a ride by pawnbrokers and unscrupulous money lenders. The only difference is that today's victims don't, as a rule, end up eating crusts of bread and entertaining mice in some dingy debtors' prison. (See also LOAN SHARK.)

V

VALUE ADDED TAX
Invented by the French, way back in 1954, as an effective and relatively painless way of taxing goods and services. Britain is switching over to it in April 1973, and the US administration is said to be "weighing the pros and cons."

Basically the VAT system collects a percentage of the price that is added to a product at each stage of manufacture and marketing. In other words, the money is collected in installments — a little bit from everybody involved in producing each item, as it moves from raw material, or someone's drawing board, through to the final consumer.

Time magazine has given the following theoretical example. A lumber mill produces a load of wood with a market price of $25; this price represents practically all the value that the mill has added to the raw timber by buying and converting it to lumber. On a VAT of 3 per cent the mill pays the government 75¢. This cost, separately invoiced, is tacked to the price of the lumber, which is then sold to a cabinetmaker for $25.75. The manufacturer transforms the lumber into a cabinet, increasing its market value from $25 to $75. On the $50 value added, the cabinetmaker pays another 3 per cent, or $1.50. When selling the cabinet to a wholesaler, he will add to the price his own tax cost, plus the 75¢ VAT that he paid the mill. The wholesaler will pass on his own tax costs along to the retailer in the same way. Ultimately the 3 per cent tax is absorbed by the consumer, so that a cabinet with a normal retail price of $100 would cost $103.

The chief attraction of VAT to governments is that (1) the revenue is large and makes it possible to bring hitherto untaxed items into the net, (2) the cost is hidden in the price, so that it is politically easier to raise money through VAT than through higher income taxes, (3) VAT does not burden exports because, unlike direct taxes, it can be rebated under international trade rules, (4) it is almost impossible to avoid.

For the consumer, of course, VAT holds much less appeal. Critics say that it is particularly unfair to the poor and lower middle class. To soften the blow, some countries give rebates to lower-income groups. There has also been talk, in Washington, of using VAT revenues to help pay for public schooling costs and to reduce the present heavy — and increasingly unpopular — property taxes.

VENTURE CAPITAL
Finance for young developing firms in areas of high technology. Most venture capitalists — usually bankers with access to institutional funds — tend toward a rather broader view, embracing more or less any company up to the stage of flotation. The basic idea is simple: find a promising small firm, provide financial backing, and share in its success. The risks implicit in venture capital are considerably higher than those associated with more conventional forms of investment, which is why the more staid finance houses don't care for it. Many venture capital companies have failed, costing their backers large sums of money.

In the United States, where the concept of twentieth-century venture capital first developed, even the oldest and probably the most successful practitioner, American Research and Development, has barely kept pace with the Dow-Jones index since the war. Its success was due to its backing of a company, Digital Equipment Corporation, which has shown an 8000 per cent increase on the original investment. In Britain, the famous Rothschild merchant banking house has tried its hand with notable lack of success. One reason may be that European merchant banks are too much bankers and not enough industrialists; venture capital situations often have to be made to work through the guidance of a central management service rather than left to their own devices.

VICIOUS CIRCLE
Action and reaction that intensify each other in a harmful way. Inflation, for example, will usually lead to more inflation — because workers, in order to make up for higher prices, will use their bargaining power to get more money,

which in turn will force employers to put up prices yet again. Poor countries, too, tend to be caught up in a vicious circle: they don't make adequate use of resources, and because they don't make adequate use of resources they cannot provide investment for further development, and because they cannot provide investment for further development they continue to make inadequate use of resources. If you see what I mean.

W

WAGE DRIFT

The gap between basic wage rates and actual earnings, which often tend to be much higher. The difference is accounted for mainly by overtime payments, bonuses, and other incentives. Extras of this kind clearly ought to figure in arguments about wage negotiations, comparisons between various jobs, and the general trend of incomes. It's surprising, though, how often economists fail to distinguish between wage rates and earnings. One good reason, of course, is that it is much easier to calculate — and understand — the effects of nationally negotiated wage rates than wages plus extras which, inevitably, vary considerably from industry to industry, trade to trade, firm to firm, and even week to week.

WARRANTS
See RIGHTS ISSUE.

WASTING ASSETS
Anything which in the foreseeable future will need to be replaced or taken out of use because it will have become worn out or obsolete. A lease on a house is a wasting asset. In industry, the term mostly refers to plant, machinery, and equipment — though it could be applied just as easily to people, including the managing director. It is an accepted principle that, in the accounts, wasting assets should be written down in value over their working life so that, subject to any residual or scrap value they may finally possess, the capital outlay at the time of purchase is recovered out of the profits earned. The amounts written off each year are known as '"depreciation."

WEALTH
To an economist, all *material* objects that have economic value. Strictly speaking, this excludes stocks, bonds, and mortgages, which are evidence of wealth, but not wealth itself. The word, in fact, is open to a great many interpretations. To Tevye, the milkman in *Fiddler on the Roof*, wealth was "a wife with a proper double chin." And there's an old Jewish ghetto story of a poor man on the bottom rung of the ladder of destitution, looking up with envy at the man just managing to retain his grip on the top rung and saying: "Oi, Oi! *There's* a rich man!" For any Socialist, of course, wealth is a dirty word. Several countries operate a wealth tax, which involves measuring a man's total worth from time to time and charging a percentage of it. In Iron Curtain countries personal wealth is condemned as antisocial, though that doesn't seem to prevent those in authority from buying themselves fancy cars and building splendid country

homes. Some people think wealth has nothing to do with money or material things; to them, health, freedom, and a good marriage all qualify for the label. Perhaps so — but don't ever try to tell that to an economist.

WIDER BANDS

As a rule, each country's paper money has a fixed value in terms of other currencies. But, of course, there are bound to be fluctuations. So there is usually a margin, a range, or, as the jargon has it, a band. The agreement among Common Market countries concluded in 1972, is, perhaps, a good example. Under it, Common Market currencies — the mark, the franc, the lira, the guilder, and so on — are allowed to fluctuate against each other by no more than 2.25 per cent. In other words, they can rise or fall by that amount before official efforts are made to keep them stable. This is a rather narrower range of fluctuation than most other countries permit, and the Common Market system was dubbed the "snake in the tunnel" of the "wider bands" accepted outside the Market. The reason is simple: it's important for everyone to know where he stands, not only because it makes trade easier but because so many Common Market schemes — such as its agricultural policy — would otherwise be in trouble. Some countries, though, are very reluctant to accept what amounts, in effect, to a monetary straitjacket. This is why one so often hears talk of the need for wider bands, or "exchange rate flexibility." Britain, although committed to joining the Market, brushed aside the EEC deal when it decided to float the pound in 1972. (See also FLOATING, FIXED PARITY, and DEVALUATION.)

WISE MEN

Any group of people charged by governments to find out where we're going, or to study the implications of some particular scheme. A journalistic term, designed to impress readers with the importance of the team. The "wise men" are often economists, and their reports tend to be weighty documents. The results, alas, are usually less impressive. "Many a crown of wisdom," American writer Paul Eldridge once said, "is but the golden chamberpot of success, worn with pompous dignity." Yes.

WORKERS' CONTROL

A popular concept, based on the unshakable conviction that all would be well if only management would step aside and let union officers have a go. In Britain, the notion goes back to the Industrial Revolution. There have been quite a number of experiments, and nearly all of them have failed. As a rule, the failures simply reflect a determined refusal to face unpalatable financial facts. Never mind if a factory cannot sell the stuff it makes, production must be maintained regardless. The state can be relied upon to foot the bill.

There would be a great deal less enthusiasm for the idea of workers' control if one suggested that workers should run, say, the coal industry as an independent, unsubsidized operation. There is nothing to stop the unions, with their millions in stocks and shares, taking over an industrial company and showing the world that they can, indeed, do better. But it does not suit them to do so. One very good reason is that the present system gives them far more effective "control": union strength is such that few managements dare brush aside the union officers' wishes. Another is that the workers themselves are skeptical; they are less interested in idealism than in the financial backing for their weekly pay envelopes. It suits them to have bosses to complain to, and to have shop stewards complain on their behalf. They don't want to be their own bosses.

It is even questionable whether the majority of workers are all that keen on nationalization. State ownership very often is a bigger foe than private enterprise. The strength of a skilled worker lies in his ability to swap jobs; state ownership reduces the range of choice.

Some people would, of course, argue that this is only so under a capitalist system. But communism is worse. Officially the worker controls Soviet industry. In practice, he does nothing of the sort. If he works for, say, the railways he finds that control is firmly in the hands of the managerial class, itself dominated by the Moscow bureaucratic class. Not only is the worker far removed from real power, but the elaborate pretense that industry is being managed in his name deprives him of the right to use his most effective weapon — the strike. It is "not necessary." There's a popular Russian joke which asks: "You know the difference between capitalism and socialism?" Answer: "Capitalism means exploitation of man by his fellow man. In socialism, it's precisely the other way around . . ."

WORLD BANK

Perhaps the most imposing name in banking. Its formal name is The International Bank for Reconstruction and Development, which is more pompous and long winded than World Bank but rather less misleading. The bank's customers are nations and no borrower ever walks away with cash in his pocket.

The World Bank was founded, together with the International Monetary Fund, in the resort town of Bretton Woods, New Hampshire, in 1944. One of its original mandates was to help finance the reconstruction of Europe following World War II, but when the United States established the Marshall Plan the bank turned to the development side of its task. The bank and its affiliates have tended to concentrate on financing specific projects in public utilities, transportation, agriculture, industry — and, more recently, education projects, tourism, and family planning. In 1956, the bank made world headlines when it withdrew from a commitment to help finance the Aswan Dam following pressure from the American and British governments. The episode is nowadays remembered with some sense of shame; "We wouldn't do it again," says one senior official.

Originally, the bank's funds came from the capital subscriptions of its members, whose percentage of ownership is related to their national income and position in world trade. Today it gets its funds mainly from the sale of its bonds in the capital markets of the world and other borrowing, and from the repayment of earlier loans. The bonds are bought by central banks, pension and trust funds, insurance companies, and other private investors. Conscious of the need to maintain a high reputation, the bank keeps a close watch on countries which secure a loan: teams of experts make careful on-the-spot investigations before it parts with any money, and the watch continues once a project is under way.

Left-wing critics say the World Bank is a capitalist tool for "structuring the global market for private gain." Bank officials claim it is a development agency dedicated to narrowing the gap between rich and poor. The one is consistent with the other. Ideal or not, the bank has certainly played a useful role in alleviating hardship.

Y

YANKEE, GO HOME

Europe's answer to what French author Jean-Jacques Schreiber called "the American challenge." Usually found scrawled on walls of American-owned plants, or chanted by militant labor unionists. Heard most loudly whenever a visiting US industrialist breaks an unwritten rule drummed into every American sent to colonize the industrial wastelands of Europe: beat them, cheat them, outsmart them, but never tell the Europeans what you really think of their goddam methods. Executives working in Europe usually obey it; the brashness of the immediate postwar years has been replaced by polite caution. They are "guests" in a foreign country, and their corporation's cause is thought to be best served if they help to smooth the susceptibilities of the natives. Most corporations go out of their way to identify themselves with the "host country." They appoint British (or French, or German) directors and, wherever possible, retain the traditional local names. What, you might ask, could be more British than Campbell's soups, British Wire Products, Britannia Lead Company, British Typewriters, and British United Shoe Machinery? They are all owned by Americans.

Economists acknowledge that US investment has done a

lot for Britain. It has provided much-needed employment in areas neglected by British companies, and has made a useful contribution to the modernization of British industry. American firms bring not just capital, but new manufacturing processes and the latest management techniques. If the government were to suppress US investment, it would simply move elsewhere. But why should it? American companies operating here are as much subject to British rules and regulations as everyone else, and their ability to dictate events should not be overrated. Nor should one exaggerate their desire to ride roughshod over local customs and government policies. But even if they did try to ride roughshod over local customs, should we consider it such a bad thing? Some of our customs deserve no better. And the deeply ingrained European habit of seeing everything in nationalist terms looks increasingly old-fashioned. It has certainly helped the Americans: it is they who leap across frontiers and create powerful multinational corporations, they who are pushing Europe into the direction it logically ought to go.

Z

ZERO GROWTH
Nothing. Nil. No progress of any kind. Trust economists, though, to find a fancy way of saying it.

FURTHER READING

Further Reading

There is no shortage of economics textbooks, but most of them are of little use to the layman. Here's a list of books which I personally would recommend to anyone who is put off by excessive use of jargon, but nevertheless wants to take a closer look at economics and finance.

Corporate Etiquette, by Milla Alihan; Weybright and Talley
The Juggernauts, by Graham Bannock; The Bobbs-Merrill Company
Welcome to the Conglomerate — You're Fired!, by Isadore Barmash; Delacorte Press
The Price of Economic Freedom, by Samuel Brittan; St. Martin's Press
Steering the Economy, by Samuel Brittan; Pelican Books
What Economics Is About, by Michael Barratt Brown; Weidenfeld and Nicolson
Business As a Game, by Albert Z. Carr; New American Library
A Popular History of Taxation, by James Coffield; Longman
The Age of Discontinuity, by Peter F. Drucker; Harper and Row, Publishers
The Infiltrators, by Nicholas Faith; E. P. Dutton and Company
Swiss Banks, by T. R. Fehrenbach; McGraw-Hill Book Company
Money-Men of Europe, by Paul Ferris; Macmillan Company
The Affluent Society, by J. K. Galbraith; Houghton Mifflin Company

The New Industrial State, by J. K. Galbraith; Houghton Mifflin Company
The World of Gold, by Timothy Green; Simon and Schuster
The Naked Manager, by Robert Heller; Barrie & Jenkins
Success Through a Positive Mental Attitude, by Napoleon Hill and W. Clement Stone; Prentice-Hall
Do You Sincerely Want to Be Rich?, by Godfrey Hodgson et al.; Viking Press
What Shall I Do with My Money?, by Eliot Janeway; David McKay Company
Corporation Man, by Anthony Jay; Random House
Management and Machiavelli, by Anthony Jay; Holt, Rinehart, and Winston
The Robber Barons, by Matthew Josephson; Harcourt Brace Jovanovitch
Managing Your Family Finances, by Jacob K. Lasser; Doubleday and Company
Playboy's Investment Guide, by Michael Laurence; Playboy Press
The Exceptional Executive, by Harry Levinson; Harvard University Press
The Managers, by Roy Lewis and Rosemary Stewart; New American Library
Business Meetings That Make Business, by John Lobingier; Macmillan Company
The American Take-Over of Britain, by James McMillan and Bernard Harris; Hart Publishing Company
Credit Cardsmanship, by Martin J. Meyer; Hawthorn Books
Twenty-one Popular Economic Fallacies, by E. J. Mishan; Praeger Publishers
A History of Money, by E. V. Morgan; Pelican Books
The Rothschilds, by Frederic Morton; Fawcett World Library
Great Myths of Economics, by Robert Paarlberg; New American Library
Do It the Hard Way, by Keith Richardson; Weidenfeld and Nicolson
Anatomy of Europe, by Anthony Sampson; Harper and Row, Publishers

The Money Game, by Adam Smith; Random House
Corporations in Crisis, by Richard Austen Smith; Doubleday and Company
How to Read the Financial News, by C. Norman Stabler; Harper and Row, Publishers
The Funny Money Game, by Andrew Tobias; Playboy Press
Up the Organization, by Robert Townsend; Fawcett World Library
Financing American Enterprise, by Paul B. Trescott; Harper and Row, Publishers
Nothing Certain but Tax, by John Turing; Hodder & Stoughton
The Merchant Bankers, by Joseph Wechsberg; Little, Brown, and Company.
And my own two books: *Merger Mania*, Constable; and *Three Years Hard Labour*, Houghton Mifflin Company.